Heels of the Ring

400 Fun Facts

About Wrestling's

Most Notorious Villains

Exploring the Drama and Legacy of Professional Wrestling's Greatest Bad Guys

Published By: Jett Clark

Heels of the Ring

Copyright Page

Copyright © 2025 by Jett Clark

All rights reserved. This book or any portion thereof may not be reproduced or used in any manner whatsoever without the express written permission of the publisher except for the use of brief quotations in a book review or scholarly journal.

This is a work of nonfiction. While the author has made every effort to ensure the accuracy of the information herein, the author assumes no responsibility for errors, omissions, or changes to factual details after publication.

Published by Jett Clark via Amazon KDP

First Printing: January 2025

Printed in the United States of America

Table of Contents

The Art of Villainy _____ 6

   The Greatest Heels of All Time _____ 10

   Iconic Betrayals _____ 17

   Cheating to Win: _____ 22

   Villains and Their Dirty Tricks _____ 22

   Cowardly Heels: _____ 27

   When Running Away Was the Strategy _____ 27

   Villainous Promos: _____ 33

   Words That Cut Deep _____ 33

   Foreign Menaces: _____ 40

   Villains Who Represented Nations _____ 40

   The Role of Managers: _____ 47

   Villainous Puppet Masters _____ 47

   The Most Disgusting Villains in Wrestling _____ 56

   Goofy Villains: _____ 63

   Characters Rejected by Fans _____ 63

   Shortest Heel Runs: _____ 68

   Villains Who Didn't Last _____ 68

   Villain Turns Rejected by Fans _____ 71

Weapons of Destruction _____ 75

   When Villains Went Too Far: _____ 85

   Real Injuries Caused by Heels _____ 85

   Psychological Weapons: _____ 93

Mind Games Before the Fight _____ 93
Vehicular Villainy: Destruction on Wheels _____ 97
Carnage in Hardcore Wrestling _____ 102
Early Characters of Notorious Wrestling Villains ____ 107
Jobber Villains: _____ 110
The Stars Who Rarely Won _____ 110
Wrestling Announcers Who Supported Villains _____ 115
Celebrity Showdowns with Villains _____ 119

Wrestling's Villainous History _____ *125*

Golden Age of Wrestling Villains _____ 128
The Evolution of Villains in the 80s & 90s _____ 133
The Modern-Day Heel: _____ 137
Villainy in the PG Era _____ 137
The Rise of Anti-Heroes _____ 141
How Villains Reflect Society's Fears _____ 145
Villains Outside the Ring: _____ 149
Public Scandals and Controversies _____ 149
Infamous Feuds: _____ 155
When Villains Took It Too Far? _____ 155
Villains Who Became Heroes _____ 160

Villain Archetypes _____ *165*

The Arrogant Villain: _____ 168
Flaunting Wealth and Power _____ 168
The Sadistic Villain: _____ 172

Thriving on Pain and Suffering 172
The Cowardly Villain: 176
Avoiding Conflict at All Costs 176
The Foreign Threat: 180
Playing on National Fears 180
The Monster Heel: 184
Destroying Everything in Their Path 184
The Charismatic Villain: 188
Winning with Words 188
Villains Who Blurred the Lines: 192
Anti-Hero Heels 192
The Comedy Villain: 196
When Evil Was Played for Laughs 196

Beyond the Ring 200

Wrestling Villains in Pop Culture 202
Villains in Wrestling Movies and TV Shows 208
Merchandising the Villain: 214
Toys, Shirts, and More 214
Real-Life Jail Time: 219
Villains Who Broke the Law 219
Fan Interactions: When the Hate Got Real 223

The Art of Villainy

In professional wrestling, the villain—the "heel"—isn't just a character; it's a masterfully crafted art form. Heels are the ones who break the rules, betray trust, and revel in the hatred of the crowd. Without these antagonists, wrestling wouldn't be the same. Every great hero needs a villain to push them to their limits, creating unforgettable stories that keep fans coming back for more. Wrestling thrives on the clash of good versus evil, and heels are the architects of that conflict.

Being a great heel, however, takes more than cheating or bending the rules. The most memorable villains are those who understand the psychology of the audience, skillfully manipulating emotions with every word and action. Whether it is Ric Flair's boastful arrogance, Roddy Piper's unpredictable insults, or MJF's scathing verbal jabs, heels have an almost magical ability to turn cheers into jeers. They make fans believe, if only for a moment, that they're witnessing something real—and they do it so convincingly that we can't help but react.

Throughout wrestling history, villains have evolved to reflect the fears, frustrations, and fascinations of their times. In the golden age of wrestling, they were often larger-than-life caricatures: foreign menaces like The Iron Sheik and Nikolai Volkoff capitalized on political tensions, while characters like Ted DiBiase flaunted their wealth in the face of hardworking fans. These heels were unapologetically one-dimensional, designed to unify the audience against them and elevate the heroic good guys.

As wrestling moved into the modern era, villainy became more layered and sophisticated. Characters like Ric Flair, Chris Jericho, and MJF blurred the line between reality and fiction, combining charisma, wit, and ruthless cunning to capture the audience's attention. These heels didn't just make us boo—they made us think, laugh, and sometimes even begrudgingly admire their brilliance. They are villains we love to hate—or sometimes even hate to love.

Heels of the Ring

But what exactly makes a great heel? Is it their ability to cheat and still win, as Eddie Guerrero famously did with his "lie, cheat, and steal" mantra? Is it their knack for delivering a promo so scathing it silences the crowd, like Jake "The Snake" Roberts' icy warnings? Or is it their willingness to embrace cowardice, avoiding conflict like The Miz or Larry Zbyszko, only to strike when the time is right? The truth is, the best heels master all of these elements and more, balancing cunning with cowardice, arrogance with charm, and rule-breaking with undeniable skill.

In this section, we'll explore the many faces of villainy in wrestling. We'll begin with some of the greatest heels of all time, from the flamboyant Ric Flair to the modern-day provocateur MJF. We'll relive iconic betrayals, like Shawn Michaels superkicking Marty Jannetty and Hulk Hogan's shocking heel turn to join the nWo. We'll uncover the psychology behind a great heel turn and examine the dirty tricks that heels use to outwit their opponents, from Mr. Fuji's salt to Ric Flair's brass knuckles.

We'll also delve into the role of managers—those devious masterminds like Bobby Heenan and Paul Heyman, who orchestrate chaos from the sidelines. And we won't forget the cowardly antics that make heels so frustrating yet entertaining, whether it's Chris Jericho hiding in an Elimination Chamber pod or The Big Show inexplicably fleeing from much smaller opponents.

The heels featured in this section aren't just bad—they're exceptional at being bad. They've mastered the art of creating drama, provoking reactions, and elevating the heroes they face. As you step into their world, remember that behind every great villain is an equally great performance. These are the characters who made us boo, hiss, and sometimes cheer—whether we wanted to or not.

Welcome to the art of villainy, where breaking the rules isn't just allowed—it's celebrated. Let the boos begin.

The Greatest Heels of All Time

Ric Flair Declares, "To Be the Man, You've Got to Beat the Man": Ric Flair's iconic catchphrase wasn't just a boast—it was a taunt aimed at challengers to his NWA World Heavyweight Championship. In a 1986 promo, Flair mocked Dusty Rhodes, claiming Rhodes could never handle the spotlight like "The Nature Boy."

Roddy Piper's Coconut Speech on Piper's Pit: Piper's infamous promo with Jimmy Snuka in 1984 escalated when Piper insulted Snuka's heritage before smashing a coconut over his head. Piper's venomous words, paired with the shocking assault, solidified his reputation as one of wrestling's most unfiltered villains.

Jake "The Snake" Roberts' Cold Words to Randy Savage: After unleashing his cobra on Savage in 1991, Roberts delivered a chilling promo, warning Savage that "trust is a weakness." His icy delivery made the feud feel deeply personal and highlighted Roberts' manipulative nature.

Hollywood Hogan's nWo Manifesto (1996): After turning heel at *Bash at the Beach*, Hogan declared the fans were the reason he had abandoned his heroic image. His speech mocked the audience for turning on him, branding himself as the leader of the New World Order.

Chris Jericho's "You Just Made the List!": Jericho's comically villainous gimmick in 2016 revolved around him keeping a list of enemies. During one segment, Jericho chastised an audience member for interrupting him, adding them to his list. This lighthearted but cutting promo made Jericho a fan-favorite heel.

Vince McMahon's "Bret Screwed Bret" (1997): After the Montreal Screwjob, McMahon delivered a cold, detached interview where he placed the blame for the incident squarely on Bret Hart. His unapologetic demeanor enraged fans and marked the beginning of his infamous Mr. McMahon character.

MJF Insults CM Punk's Legacy (2022): In a scathing promo on AEW, MJF called CM Punk a "quitter," accusing him of abandoning wrestling when it got tough. The promo hit a nerve, as MJF intertwined real-life criticism with kayfabe, blurring the lines between fiction and reality.

Freddie Blassie's "Pencil-Neck Geeks": Blassie's go-to insult became a staple of his promos in the 1960s and 1970s. In one particularly memorable tirade, Blassie mocked both his opponent and the audience, labeling everyone "pencil-neck geeks" incapable of understanding greatness.

The Iron Sheik's Anti-American Rants: Sheik's promos often targeted American heroes like Hulk Hogan and Sgt. Slaughter. In a 1984 promo, he called the U.S. "a land of weaklings," vowing to bring glory to Iran. His fiery speeches drew intense boos and solidified him as a top foreign heel.

Randy Orton's "Legend Killer" Declaration: During his feud with Mick Foley in 2004, Orton delivered a promo calling Foley a "washed-up has-been" who didn't belong in the same ring as him. Orton's smug delivery fueled his rise as a hated villain.

Logan Paul Mocks the WWE Universe (2022): Paul's promo against The Miz on *Raw* accused fans of being jealous of his success outside wrestling. His cocky delivery and refusal to acknowledge the audience's boos reinforced his outsider persona.

Superstar Billy Graham's "I'm the Reflection of Perfection": Graham's promos in the 1970s were filled with rhymes and boasts about his physique. In one promo, he claimed, "I'm too sweet to be sour, the women love me, and the men want to be me," drawing heat for his arrogance.

Mr. Perfect's Perfect Life: Curt Hennig's promos revolved around his supposed perfection. In one skit, he bragged about his ability to bowl a perfect game, hit a hole-in-one in golf, and beat anyone in the ring. His flawless persona made him an easy target for fan ire.

Jake Roberts on Trust: During his feud with The Undertaker in 1992, Roberts delivered a cryptic promo, warning Taker that "you can't trust anyone, especially me." The line underscored Roberts' cunning and set the tone for their WrestleMania VIII match.

Mick McManus' Snobbish Rants (1970s): British wrestling villain McManus would often mock working-class fans, claiming they didn't deserve to see him wrestle. In one famous promo, he refused to shake hands with his opponent, citing them as "beneath" him.

Gorgeous George's "Human Orchid" Monologues: George's promos in the 1950s were theatrical performances, where he described himself as a "flower among weeds." His over-the-top delivery infuriated audiences and inspired generations of villains.

The Fabulous Moolah Belittles Rivals: Moolah's promos focused on mocking her opponents, often calling them "weak girls" who didn't belong in the ring. Her patronizing tone during a 1983 segment against Wendi Richter turned fans firmly against her.

Kevin Owens Calls Out "Hypocrite" Fans: During his feud with John Cena in 2015, Owens delivered a promo accusing fans of cheering for Cena despite knowing he was holding younger talent back. His scathing words blurred kayfabe and reality, earning him heat.

Tiger Jeet Singh's Sword-Wielding Tirades: Singh often brandished his sword during promos, threatening opponents and even the audience. In a 1979 promo in Japan, he vowed to "cut through anyone who disrespects me," drawing massive heat.

Bret Hart's Anti-American Rant (1997): During his heel turn in 1997, Hart lambasted American fans for cheering "degenerates" like Shawn Michaels. His bitter promos during this period turned him into a national hero in Canada while making him a villain in the U.S.

Iconic Betrayals

Hulk Hogan Turns Heel (1996): At *Bash at the Beach 1996*, Hulk Hogan stunned the wrestling world by turning on Randy Savage and aligning with The Outsiders. Hogan's leg drop on Savage solidified the formation of the nWo and marked one of the most shocking betrayals in wrestling history.

Shawn Michaels Kicks Marty Jannetty: The infamous Barber Shop segment saw Shawn Michaels superkick his longtime tag team partner Marty Jannetty, sending him crashing through a glass window. This moment launched Michaels' solo career and became one of wrestling's most iconic betrayals.

Heels of the Ring

Seth Rollins Turns on The Shield (2014): Rollins shocked fans when he attacked Roman Reigns and Dean Ambrose with a steel chair, aligning himself with The Authority. This betrayal marked the beginning of Rollins' ascent as a top heel in WWE.

Stone Cold Aligns with Vince McMahon (2001): At *WrestleMania X-Seven*, Stone Cold Steve Austin shook hands with Vince McMahon after defeating The Rock for the WWF Championship. The partnership marked a stunning betrayal of Austin's anti-authority persona.

Andre the Giant Joins Bobby Heenan (1987): Andre's decision to side with Bobby Heenan and challenge Hulk Hogan for the WWF Championship at *WrestleMania III* broke fans' hearts. The betrayal set up one of the most legendary matches in wrestling history.

Chris Jericho's Attack on Kevin Owens (2017): During the "Festival of Friendship" segment on *Raw*, Jericho's heartfelt gift to Owens was met with betrayal as Owens viciously attacked him, ending their alliance. The segment became an instant classic.

Ric Flair Turns on Sting (1995): Flair's betrayal of Sting during their match against Arn Anderson and Brian Pillman was a masterclass in deception. Flair's feigned alliance with Sting set up yet another chapter in their storied rivalry.

Triple H Betrays Randy Orton (2004): After helping Orton win the World Heavyweight Championship, Triple H turned on him, delivering a brutal beatdown with Evolution. The betrayal marked Orton's transition to a solo career.

Dominik Mysterio Turns on Rey (2022): Dominik's shocking attack on his father Rey Mysterio at *Clash at the Castle* cemented his heel turn. The emotional betrayal was fueled by jealousy and led to one of the most personal rivalries in WWE.

Paul Bearer Turns on The Undertaker (1996): During Undertaker's match against Mankind at *SummerSlam 1996*, Paul

Bearer struck The Undertaker with the urn, aligning himself with Mankind. The betrayal shocked fans and added new layers to the Deadman's character.

CM Punk Turns on The Rock (2013): After months of tension, CM Punk attacked The Rock during a segment on *Raw*, signaling his allegiance to Paul Heyman. The betrayal reignited Punk's feud with WWE management and the fans.

Randy Orton's RKO on Ric Flair (2020): During a *Raw* segment, Orton shockingly delivered an RKO to his mentor Ric Flair after feigning respect. The betrayal highlighted Orton's ruthless persona as "The Legend Killer."

Jake Roberts Betrays Ultimate Warrior (1991): Roberts lured Warrior into a series of traps orchestrated by The Undertaker, culminating in a shocking betrayal. Roberts' mind games added a psychological edge to their feud.

MJF Betrays Cody Rhodes (2019): MJF's low blow to Cody Rhodes at *Full Gear* ended their alliance and turned MJF into one of AEW's top heels. The betrayal felt deeply personal, leaving fans furious.

Logan Paul Betrays The Miz (2022): After teaming with The Miz at *WrestleMania 38*, Logan Paul turned on him during a *Raw* segment, setting the stage for their feud. Paul's betrayal drew massive heat from the crowd.

Cheating to Win:

Villains and Their Dirty Tricks

Ric Flair's Brass Knuckles: Ric Flair was infamous for hiding brass knuckles in his tights, which he used to knock out opponents when the referee's back was turned. This sneaky tactic helped him retain countless championships and solidify his reputation as the ultimate dirtiest player in the game.

Eddie Guerrero's Lie, Cheat, and Steal: Eddie Guerrero's antics included pretending to be hit by a chair and throwing it to his opponent, fooling referees into disqualifying them. His ability to bend the rules with charm turned his heelish cheating into a beloved trademark.

The Mountie's Cattle Prod: The Mountie carried an electric cattle prod, using it to incapacitate opponents behind the referee's back. This shocking weapon became synonymous with his reign of terror as Intercontinental Champion in the early 1990s.

Triple H's Sledgehammer: Triple H's infamous sledgehammer became his signature weapon, often used to deliver devastating blows during high-stakes matches. In his rivalry with The Rock, he capitalized on referee distractions to ensure victory with the forbidden weapon.

Mr. Fuji's Salt Toss: Mr. Fuji was notorious for throwing salt into the eyes of his clients' opponents, blinding them and allowing his wrestlers to capitalize. This tactic helped Yokozuna win the WWF Championship at *WrestleMania IX*.

Heels of the Ring

Jake Roberts' Snake Distractions: Jake "The Snake" Roberts would often unleash his python, Damien, to terrify and distract opponents. In one iconic moment, he placed Damien on a fallen Randy Savage, paralyzing him with fear and securing victory.

The Iron Sheik's Loaded Boot: The Iron Sheik would discreetly load his boot by kicking it against the mat, then deliver a devastating kick to his opponent. This trick was a key part of his arsenal during his heated rivalry with Sgt. Slaughter.

Chris Jericho's Foot on the Ropes: Jericho was infamous for using the ropes for leverage during pinfalls. In his 2001 match against The Rock, Jericho secured the Undisputed Championship by using this underhanded tactic when the referee wasn't looking.

Ted DiBiase's Bribery: "The Million Dollar Man" Ted DiBiase famously tried to buy championships and even hired crooked referees. His attempt to purchase the WWF

Championship from Andre the Giant highlighted his willingness to cheat at all costs.

Shawn Michaels Fakes an Injury: During his 1997 rivalry with The Undertaker, Michaels faked a knee injury to distract officials and land Sweet Chin Music for the win. His ability to play possum was key to many of his victories.

The Miz's Foot on the Ropes for Leverage: The Miz frequently used the ropes to apply extra pressure during submissions or pinfalls. This tactic was instrumental in his successful defense of the WWE Championship against John Cena in 2011.

Vickie Guerrero's Restart Shenanigans: Vickie Guerrero, as SmackDown General Manager, often abused her power by restarting matches in favor of her clients like Edge. Her favoritism and interference made her one of the most reviled managers in WWE history.

Heels of the Ring

Santino Marella's Cobra Tactics: While comedic, Santino's "Cobra" hand puppet was a deceptive move that often turned the tide in matches. By distracting opponents with its absurdity, he caught many off-guard to secure victories.

Harvey Wippleman's Interference for Giant Gonzales: During Gonzales' feud with The Undertaker, Wippleman constantly interfered, from distracting referees to tossing foreign objects into the ring. His antics ensured Gonzales maintained an edge in their encounters.

The Fabulous Freebirds' Freebird Rule: This infamous rule allowed any two members of a trio to defend their tag team titles, confusing opponents and giving the Freebirds a strategic advantage. The rule has since been adopted by several heel factions.

Cowardly Heels:

When Running Away Was the Strategy

The Honky Tonk Man's Escapes: During his record-breaking Intercontinental Championship reign, Honky Tonk Man frequently retained his title by intentionally getting himself counted out or disqualified. A master of evasion, he would feign injuries, slip out of the ring at opportune moments, or provoke his opponents into breaking the rules. His reluctance to engage in fair competition frustrated fans, who clamored for a hero to dethrone him.

Heels of the Ring

Hollywood Hogan's Retreats from Sting: Throughout the buildup to *Starrcade 1997*, Hollywood Hogan perfected the art of avoidance. Sting's silent menace loomed large, but Hogan repeatedly fled from physical confrontations, often hiding behind nWo allies like Scott Hall and Kevin Nash. These calculated retreats heightened the audience's anticipation for Sting's eventual retribution.

Larry Zbyszko's Stalling Tactics: Known as "The Living Legend," Zbyszko was infamous for his stalling and retreating during matches, especially in his heated feud with Bruno Sammartino. He would roll out of the ring, argue with fans, or plead with referees to buy himself time. These antics not only enraged the crowd but also added drama to every match he wrestled.

MJF's Fake Injuries: A master manipulator, MJF has frequently faked injuries to gain sympathy or delay matches. During his rivalry with Jon Moxley, he arrived at a contract signing wearing a neck brace, only to reveal his deception moments later. His ability to blend cowardice with cunning tactics makes him one of AEW's most compelling villains.

Chris Jericho's Elimination Chamber Hideout: In a 2010 Elimination Chamber match, Jericho avoided confrontation by staying locked inside his pod for as long as possible. When his pod finally opened, Jericho seized the opportunity to eliminate The Undertaker, demonstrating that his strategic cowardice could still yield results.

Triple H's Avoidance of Goldberg: During Goldberg's explosive WWE run, Triple H often dodged direct confrontations, relying on Evolution members Randy Orton and Batista to do his dirty work. His refusal to face Goldberg one-on-one created tension that culminated in their eventual clashes, where Goldberg's victories provided satisfying payoffs for fans.

The Miz Hides Behind Maryse: Throughout his career, The Miz has used his wife Maryse as a human shield to escape attacks. During his feud with Dolph Ziggler in 2016, Maryse's distractions allowed Miz to slip away or gain an unfair advantage. This dynamic made him one of WWE's most detestable yet entertaining heels.

Heels of the Ring

Baron Corbin's Strategic Retreats: Corbin's tendency to slide out of the ring and regroup became a hallmark of his heel persona. In matches against Roman Reigns, he would taunt the crowd before retreating, forcing Reigns to chase him. These tactics not only frustrated opponents but also made fans eager to see him get his comeuppance.

Edge's Opportunistic Escapes: As the "Ultimate Opportunist," Edge frequently avoided battles until he could strike at the perfect moment. In 2006, during his Money in the Bank cash-in against John Cena, Edge waited for Cena to be utterly exhausted before swooping in to claim victory. His calculated cowardice made him a strategic and despised heel.

The Big Show's Unlikely Cowardice: Despite his immense size, The Big Show occasionally portrayed a cowardly heel, retreating from smaller opponents like Rey Mysterio. These moments of unexpected fear, often punctuated by exaggerated expressions, added a comedic edge to his character and made his eventual defeats even more satisfying for fans.

Heels of the Ring

Randy Orton's Tactical Exits: Orton's calculated retreats were a staple of his "Legend Killer" persona. In a 2009 feud with Kofi Kingston, Orton frequently left the ring to avoid Kingston's high-energy offense, only to return when the odds were in his favor. His ability to frustrate opponents and audiences alike showcased his mastery of psychological warfare.

Kevin Owens' Strategic Walkouts: Owens often left matches mid-way, especially when facing physically imposing opponents like Braun Strowman. These exits were not only a way to preserve himself but also a ploy to lure his opponents into overconfidence. His frequent walkouts during his Universal Championship reign amplified his role as a conniving heel.

Ric Flair's "Flop and Roll": Flair's exaggerated falls and pleading in the ring became iconic parts of his character. Often pretending to be injured or begging for mercy, Flair would use these moments to catch his breath or lure opponents into a false sense of security before launching a counterattack.

Santino Marella's Hilarious Escapes: Marella's over-the-top attempts to evade opponents were a comedic highlight of his matches. Whether he was diving out of the ring or crawling under it, his exaggerated cowardice added levity to WWE programming while still making him a detestable heel in critical moments.

Elias Avoids Braun Strowman: During their feud, Elias repeatedly fled from Braun Strowman's overwhelming strength. He would taunt Strowman with songs and insults, only to bolt as soon as the Monster Among Men approached. These antics built anticipation for the inevitable moments when Strowman finally got his hands on Elias.

Villainous Promos:

Words That Cut Deep

Ric Flair Declares, "To Be the Man, You've Got to Beat the Man": Ric Flair's iconic catchphrase wasn't just a boast—it was a taunt aimed at challengers to his NWA World Heavyweight Championship. In a 1986 promo, Flair mocked Dusty Rhodes, claiming Rhodes could never handle the spotlight like "The Nature Boy."

Heels of the Ring

Roddy Piper's Coconut Speech on Piper's Pit: Piper's infamous promo with Jimmy Snuka in 1984 escalated when Piper insulted Snuka's heritage before smashing a coconut over his head. Piper's venomous words, paired with the shocking assault, solidified his reputation as one of wrestling's most unfiltered villains.

Jake "The Snake" Roberts' Cold Words to Randy Savage: After unleashing his cobra on Savage in 1991, Roberts delivered a chilling promo, warning Savage that "trust is a weakness." His icy delivery made the feud feel deeply personal and highlighted Roberts' manipulative nature.

Hollywood Hogan's nWo Manifesto (1996): After turning heel at *Bash at the Beach*, Hogan declared the fans were the reason he had abandoned his heroic image. His speech mocked the audience for turning on him, branding himself as the leader of the New World Order.

Chris Jericho's "You Just Made the List!": Jericho's comically villainous gimmick in 2016 revolved around him keeping a list of enemies. During one segment, Jericho chastised an audience member for interrupting him, adding them to his list. This lighthearted but cutting promo made Jericho a fan-favorite heel.

Vince McMahon's "Bret Screwed Bret" (1997): After the Montreal Screwjob, McMahon delivered a cold, detached interview where he placed the blame for the incident squarely on Bret Hart. His unapologetic demeanor enraged fans and marked the beginning of his infamous Mr. McMahon character.

MJF Insults CM Punk's Legacy (2022): In a scathing promo on AEW, MJF called CM Punk a "quitter," accusing him of abandoning wrestling when it got tough. The promo hit a nerve, as MJF intertwined real-life criticism with kayfabe, blurring the lines between fiction and reality.

Freddie Blassie's "Pencil-Neck Geeks": Blassie's go-to insult became a staple of his promos in the 1960s and 1970s. In one particularly memorable tirade, Blassie mocked both his opponent and the audience, labeling everyone "pencil-neck geeks" incapable of understanding greatness.

The Iron Sheik's Anti-American Rants: Sheik's promos often targeted American heroes like Hulk Hogan and Sgt. Slaughter. In a 1984 promo, he called the U.S. "a land of weaklings," vowing to bring glory to Iran. His fiery speeches drew intense boos and solidified him as a top foreign heel.

Randy Orton's "Legend Killer" Declaration: During his feud with Mick Foley in 2004, Orton delivered a promo calling Foley a "washed-up has-been" who didn't belong in the same ring as him. Orton's smug delivery fueled his rise as a hated villain.

Logan Paul Mocks the WWE Universe (2022): Paul's promo against The Miz on *Raw* accused fans of being jealous of his success outside wrestling. His cocky delivery and refusal to acknowledge the audience's boos reinforced his outsider persona.

Superstar Billy Graham's "I'm the Reflection of Perfection": Graham's promos in the 1970s were filled with rhymes and boasts about his physique. In one promo, he claimed, "I'm too sweet to be sour, the women love me, and the men want to be me," drawing heat for his arrogance.

Mr. Perfect's Perfect Life: Curt Hennig's promos revolved around his supposed perfection. In one skit, he bragged about his ability to bowl a perfect game, hit a hole-in-one in golf, and beat anyone in the ring. His flawless persona made him an easy target for fan ire.

Jake Roberts on Trust: During his feud with The Undertaker in 1992, Roberts delivered a cryptic promo, warning Taker that "you can't trust anyone, especially me." The line underscored Roberts' cunning and set the tone for their WrestleMania VIII match.

Mick McManus' Snobbish Rants (1970s): British wrestling villain McManus would often mock working-class fans, claiming they didn't deserve to see him wrestle. In one famous promo, he refused to shake hands with his opponent, citing them as "beneath" him.

Gorgeous George's "Human Orchid" Monologues: George's promos in the 1950s were theatrical performances, where he described himself as a "flower among weeds." His over-the-top delivery infuriated audiences and inspired generations of villains.

The Fabulous Moolah Belittles Rivals: Moolah's promos focused on mocking her opponents, often calling them "weak girls" who didn't belong in the ring. Her patronizing tone during a 1983 segment against Wendi Richter turned fans firmly against her.

Kevin Owens Calls Out "Hypocrite" Fans: During his feud with John Cena in 2015, Owens delivered a promo accusing fans of cheering for Cena despite knowing he was holding younger talent back. His scathing words blurred kayfabe and reality, earning him heat.

Tiger Jeet Singh's Sword-Wielding Tirades: Singh often brandished his sword during promos, threatening opponents and even the audience. In a 1979 promo in Japan, he vowed to "cut through anyone who disrespects me," drawing massive heat.

Bret Hart's Anti-American Rant (1997): During his heel turn in 1997, Hart lambasted American fans for cheering "degenerates" like Shawn Michaels. His bitter promos during this period turned him into a national hero in Canada while making him a villain in the U.S.

Foreign Menaces:

Villains Who Represented Nations

The Iron Sheik and Iranian Pride: The Iron Sheik became synonymous with anti-American sentiment in the 1980s, often waving the Iranian flag before matches. His feud with Hulk Hogan in 1984 symbolized the Cold War tension between the U.S. and the Middle East, making his matches feel larger than life.

Nikolai Volkoff Sings the Soviet Anthem: Volkoff's insistence on singing the Soviet national anthem before every match was designed to enrage American audiences during the height of the Cold War. At *WrestleMania I*, he infuriated fans by teaming with The Iron Sheik to defeat The U.S. Express.

Kendo Nagasaki's Japanese Mysticism: As a masked wrestler, Kendo Nagasaki combined mysticism and Japanese traditions to mystify and intimidate his opponents. His eerie persona and use of martial arts techniques in British wrestling made him a standout heel.

Yokozuna's Samoan-Japanese Persona: Though Samoan by heritage, Yokozuna portrayed a Japanese sumo wrestler managed by Mr. Fuji. His 1993 WWF Championship win over Bret Hart at *WrestleMania IX* came after Mr. Fuji threw salt into Hart's eyes, cementing Yokozuna's status as a foreign menace.

The Fabulous Kangaroos Represent Australia: Al Costello and Roy Heffernan, known as The Fabulous Kangaroos, brought an Australian gimmick to the tag team scene. Waving boomerangs and mocking their American opponents, they became one of the first truly international heels.

William Regal and British Superiority: Regal's "Real Man's Man" persona in WWE included mocking American culture and promoting British values. His aristocratic attitude and sharp wit made him one of wrestling's most despised British villains.

Jinder Mahal as the Modern-Day Maharaja: Mahal's 2017 WWE Championship run leaned heavily on his Indian heritage. He often claimed that American fans disrespected him because of his culture, adding a layer of real-world tension to his villainous persona.

Colonel DeBeers' South African Apartheid Gimmick: In the 1980s, Colonel DeBeers portrayed a wrestler who supported apartheid, drawing massive heat. His refusal to wrestle African-American opponents in kayfabe amplified his role as a despicable villain.

El Santo's Opposite: Blue Demon: While El Santo was Mexico's beloved hero, Blue Demon played the villain. Representing the darker side of lucha libre, Blue Demon's masked persona clashed with El Santo's virtue, creating one of wrestling's most iconic rivalries.

Toru Yano's Japanese Prankster Persona: In NJPW, Toru Yano often mocks his opponents and the audience with his lighthearted but cunning antics. Representing Japan, his blend of humor and rule-breaking makes him an unconventional heel on the international stage.

Ivan Koloff Ends Bruno Sammartino's Reign: Representing the Soviet Union, Koloff became one of wrestling's most hated villains after defeating Bruno Sammartino for the WWF Championship in 1971. The shock of Sammartino's loss devastated fans, elevating Koloff's status as a Cold War-era menace.

Ultimo Dragon's Japanese Flair: While often a respected competitor, Ultimo Dragon's heel turn in WCW saw him mock

American wrestlers for their lack of discipline. His intricate costumes and Japanese heritage added depth to his villainous persona.

The Great Kabuki's Green Mist: Kabuki's use of green mist and his mysterious Japanese heritage turned him into a feared heel. During his feud with Dusty Rhodes in the 1980s, Kabuki's foreign mystique and underhanded tactics made him one of the most unique villains of the era.

Hakushi and Japanese Symbolism: Hakushi's painted body and silent demeanor made him an enigmatic figure in the WWF during the 1990s. His feud with Bret Hart showcased his technical skills and his ability to play a quiet but menacing heel.

André the Giant's French Pride: Before becoming beloved by fans, André occasionally leaned into his French heritage to antagonize American audiences. His towering presence and condescending remarks about American wrestling traditions made him an effective early heel.

La Parka's Skeleton Persona: Known as "The Chairman" of WCW, La Parka's villainous antics were tied to his lucha libre roots. His comedic but aggressive style, coupled with his Mexican heritage, made him a standout international heel.

Antonio Inoki's Feud with Muhammad Ali: Though primarily a hero in Japan, Inoki's controversial match with Ali in 1976 saw him adopt heelish tactics. His calculated use of grappling techniques frustrated American audiences, positioning him as a foreign threat.

The Bolsheviks and Soviet Domination: The tag team of Nikolai Volkoff and Boris Zhukov used their Soviet gimmick to draw massive heat during the Cold War. Their losses to American heroes like The Hart Foundation symbolized the ultimate triumph of good over evil.

Mil Máscaras' Rivalries in America: Though revered in Mexico, Mil Máscaras occasionally adopted a heel persona in the U.S., mocking American wrestlers for their lack of lucha libre prowess. His technical style and arrogance alienated American fans.

Sheamus' Irish Warrior Persona: During his 2012 heel run, Sheamus mocked American culture, claiming that Irish toughness and tradition were superior. His feud with Daniel Bryan highlighted his mix of arrogance and physical dominance.

Killer Khan's Mongolian Stomper: Khan's portrayal as a Mongolian menace in the 1980s saw him use brutal tactics like choking and stomping to defeat opponents. His feud with André the Giant included several controversial matches where Khan used underhanded tricks to gain the upper hand.

The Role of Managers:

Villainous Puppet Masters

Bobby "The Brain" Heenan's Scheming for Andre the Giant: Bobby Heenan played a pivotal role in turning Andre the Giant against Hulk Hogan in 1987. Heenan's cunning manipulation highlighted Andre's frustrations, leading to the unforgettable match at *WrestleMania III*. Heenan's vocal taunts and interference during the buildup painted Hogan as a selfish champion, setting the stage for one of wrestling's biggest betrayals.

Heels of the Ring

Paul Heyman's Advocacy for Brock Lesnar: Paul Heyman's alliance with Brock Lesnar redefined villainy in modern wrestling. At *SummerSlam 2014*, Heyman hyped Lesnar as "the conqueror of John Cena," building anticipation for Lesnar's dominant victory. Heyman's ability to weave Lesnar's brute force into compelling narratives turned their partnership into an unparalleled force of destruction.

Jimmy Hart's Megaphone Interference for The Hart Foundation: Jimmy Hart's notorious megaphone was as loud as it was dangerous. In 1986, during a match against The British Bulldogs, Hart handed the megaphone to Bret Hart and Jim Neidhart, who used it to knock out their opponents and secure a controversial victory. The move solidified their reputation as cunning champions.

Miss Elizabeth's Subtle Manipulations for Randy Savage: Miss Elizabeth's gentle demeanor often masked her influence in matches. During Randy Savage's heated rivalry with Hulk Hogan in 1989, Elizabeth's strategic positioning distracted both men, fueling the tension. Her tears and seemingly accidental interference added emotional weight to the feud, driving fans into a frenzy.

Mr. Fuji's Salt Throwing for Yokozuna: Mr. Fuji's underhanded tactics were legendary, especially during Yokozuna's WWF Championship reign. At *WrestleMania IX*, Fuji threw salt into Bret Hart's eyes, leaving him defenseless against Yokozuna's Banzai Drop. Fuji's devious methods ensured Yokozuna's dominance as champion.

Jim Cornette's Tennis Racket for The Midnight Express: Jim Cornette's tennis racket wasn't just for show—it was a weapon of choice. During a pivotal NWA match in 1986, Cornette struck The Rock 'n' Roll Express with the racket while the referee was distracted, enabling The Midnight Express to win. His sharp wit and ringside antics made him a lightning rod for fan hatred.

Sensational Sherri's Ruthless Support for Shawn Michaels: Sherri Martel's loyalty to Shawn Michaels often came with a dose of brutality. In a 1992 match against Bret Hart, Sherri struck Hart with her high heel, giving Michaels the opening he needed to secure victory. Her willingness to get physically involved highlighted her fierce devotion to her protégés.

Paul Bearer's Urn for The Undertaker: Paul Bearer's eerie presence and his mystical urn became symbols of The Undertaker's power. During *Survivor Series 1991*, Bearer dramatically raised the urn to reinvigorate The Undertaker, helping him defeat Hulk Hogan for the WWF Championship. Bearer's ghostly demeanor added an otherworldly aura to the Deadman's matches.

Freddie Blassie's Verbal Assaults for The Iron Sheik: Freddie Blassie's sharp tongue was a weapon in its own right. During The Iron Sheik's 1984 feud with Hulk Hogan, Blassie taunted Hogan and the fans, fueling the crowd's animosity. His words set the stage for Sheik's shocking title win over Bob Backlund, marking a pivotal moment in wrestling history.

Vickie Guerrero's "Excuse Me!" Power Plays for Edge: Vickie Guerrero's partnership with Edge was marked by her abuse of authority as SmackDown General Manager. During a 2008 match with The Undertaker, Guerrero restarted the match after Undertaker had seemingly won, allowing Edge to retain his championship. Her shrill catchphrase became a hallmark of her villainy.

Gary Hart's Guidance for The Great Kabuki: Gary Hart introduced The Great Kabuki and his infamous green mist to American audiences in the 1980s. During a feud with Dusty Rhodes, Kabuki blinded Rhodes with the mist, giving him an advantage. Hart's innovative strategies brought international flair to his managerial career.

The Grand Wizard's Flair for "Superstar" Billy Graham: The Grand Wizard's flamboyant style was the perfect complement to "Superstar" Billy Graham's larger-than-life persona. In 1977, Wizard's interference during a match with Bruno Sammartino helped Graham secure the WWF Championship, cementing both men as icons of the era.

Heels of the Ring

JJ Dillon's Leadership of The Four Horsemen: As the mastermind behind The Four Horsemen, JJ Dillon orchestrated calculated attacks on their rivals. During their feud with Dusty Rhodes, Dillon distracted the referee while Arn Anderson and Tully Blanchard launched a brutal double-team assault, showcasing the Horsemen's unity and cunning.

Sunny's Manipulations for The Bodydonnas: Sunny's charisma masked her devious tendencies. During The Bodydonnas' Tag Team Championship match in 1996, she distracted the referee, allowing Skip and Zip to double-team their opponents. Her tactics ensured their reign and elevated her as one of the most notorious female managers.

Luna Vachon's Ferocity for Bam Bam Bigelow: Luna Vachon's chaotic energy added a wild edge to Bam Bam Bigelow's matches. During his feud with Doink the Clown in 1994, Vachon physically attacked Doink's ally, Dink, at ringside, escalating the chaos and securing Bigelow's victory.

Freddie Blassie's Bribery for Nikolai Volkoff: Blassie's managerial cunning was on full display when he orchestrated a controversial victory for Nikolai Volkoff in 1974. By bribing a referee, Volkoff was able to escape certain defeat and secure his position as a top villain.

Harvey Wippleman's Scheming for Giant Gonzales: Harvey Wippleman's partnership with Giant Gonzales centered around ambush tactics. During Gonzales' feud with The Undertaker, Wippleman orchestrated sneak attacks that left The Undertaker vulnerable, including a brutal post-match assault at *WrestleMania IX*.

Slick's Tactics for The Twin Towers: Slick's streetwise demeanor belied his calculated interference. During a 1989 tag team match, Slick distracted the referee while Akeem and The Big Boss Man executed a devastating double slam, leading to their victory. His clever manipulation made The Twin Towers a dominant force.

Heels of the Ring

The Sheik's Fireball for Abdullah the Butcher: The Sheik's infamous fireball attack became a defining feature of his managerial career. During a 1970s match, he threw a fireball at Dusty Rhodes, allowing Abdullah the Butcher to pin Rhodes and win the bout. The shocking act left fans in disbelief.

Chyna's Muscle for Triple H and Shawn Michaels: As D-Generation X's enforcer, Chyna frequently tipped the scales in favor of Triple H and Shawn Michaels. During their feud with The Nation of Domination, Chyna delivered a low blow to The Rock, ensuring DX's victory and solidifying her role as a fearsome ally.

Jimmy Hart's Alliance with The Nasty Boys: Jimmy Hart's partnership with The Nasty Boys was built on chaos. At *WrestleMania VII*, Hart distracted the referee while Brian Knobbs and Jerry Sags used Hart's megaphone to knock out their opponents, securing the WWF Tag Team Championship.

Paul Heyman's Betrayal of CM Punk: Paul Heyman's shocking betrayal of CM Punk during the 2013 Money in the

Bank ladder match was a masterclass in treachery. By siding with Brock Lesnar, Heyman not only cost Punk the match but also demonstrated that his loyalty always lay with power.

The Most Disgusting Villains in Wrestling

George "The Animal" Steele's Turnbuckle Biting: George Steele was infamous for tearing apart turnbuckles with his teeth during matches, leaving bits of foam scattered across the ring. Fans were both repulsed and fascinated as he chewed on the stuffing, drooling all over himself before spitting it out in front of a horrified audience. His wild, animalistic behavior made him a true spectacle of disgust.

Bastion Booger's Unkempt Appearance: With his stained, torn singlet barely covering his oversized frame, Bastion

Booger looked as though hygiene was the last thing on his mind. He would often burp and pick at his food mid-match, grossing out fans and opponents alike. His persona was built on making everyone around him as uncomfortable as possible.

The Boogeyman's Worm Diet: Few could forget the horrifying image of The Boogeyman chomping down on live worms during matches or promos. He would even stuff the writhing creatures into his opponent's mouths, as he did to Jillian Hall during a SmackDown segment. The sheer shock value of his worm-eating antics made him one of wrestling's most unsettling characters.

The Mountie's Dirty Prison Cell Antics: After losing a jailhouse match to The Big Boss Man at *SummerSlam 1991*, The Mountie was locked in a cell with disheveled inmates who leered at him. The implication of his predicament was played for laughs but left fans with a lasting sense of disgust.

Doink the Clown's Water-Spitting Flower: As a heel, Doink the Clown used a squirting flower filled with foul-smelling liquid to spray at opponents and even fans. The lingering stench added an extra layer of revulsion to his otherwise comedic antics.

The Dudley Boyz and Their "Spit Milkshake": In ECW, The Dudley Boyz earned boos for mixing spit, chewed food, and other revolting substances into "milkshakes" that they poured onto defeated opponents. This tactic perfectly embodied the boundary-pushing nature of ECW's most detestable villains.

Adrian Adonis' Over-the-Top Makeup: Adonis' "Adorable" gimmick included heavy makeup that often smeared during matches, giving him an unkempt and grotesque appearance. Coupled with his flamboyant antics, Adonis drew boos and uncomfortable reactions from fans.

Goldust's "Bizarre" Tactics: In the early days of his career, Goldust frequently licked opponents' faces, breathed heavily into their ears, and made suggestive gestures mid-match. These unsettling behaviors, paired with his enigmatic persona, earned him widespread disdain and confusion.

The Great Khali's Spitting Habit: Khali was notorious for spitting huge globs of saliva into the air during his entrances. The unfortunate fans near the ramp often found themselves dodging droplets, making his entrances memorable for all the wrong reasons.

Kevin Sullivan's Satanic Gimmick: In the 1980s, Kevin Sullivan's "Prince of Darkness" gimmick involved occult rituals and unsettling imagery. During one promo, he smeared what appeared to be blood on himself and his followers, leaving fans questioning whether they were watching a wrestling show or a horror film.

Mantaur's Animalistic Behavior: Portraying a half-man, half-bull character, Mantaur grunted, snorted, and even drooled on opponents. His over-the-top antics made fans uncomfortable, and his bizarre presentation was often met with more confusion than applause.

Hugh Morrus' Spit-Take Laughs: After defeating opponents, Hugh Morrus would erupt into a maniacal laugh, often spraying spit everywhere. His exaggerated laughter, combined with the gross visual, made his celebrations as revolting as they were memorable.

Mick Foley's Sock Puppet Antics as Mankind: Mankind's finishing move, the Mandible Claw, involved him stuffing a filthy sock, "Mr. Socko," into opponents' mouths. The sock, pulled from his tights, was often portrayed as sweaty and grimy, making the move even more disgusting to watch.

Papa Shango's Curse on The Ultimate Warrior: In one of WWE's most bizarre storylines, Papa Shango "cursed" The Ultimate Warrior, causing him to vomit backstage. The unsettling visual effects, combined with the storyline's supernatural elements, left fans uncomfortable and grossed out.

Gene Snitsky's Hygiene Issues: Snitsky's greasy, yellow teeth and deliberately unclean appearance were exaggerated to make him look unsettling. His creepy behavior in promos, including leering and heavy breathing, added to his revolting image.

Big Bully Busick's Cigar Tactics: Busick often blew cigar smoke directly into opponents' faces, leaving them coughing and irritated. The combination of his smug attitude and the unpleasant smell added an extra layer of villainy.

T.L. Hopper's Plunger Antics: T.L. Hopper, portraying a wrestling plumber, used a visibly dirty plunger as a weapon. In one particularly disgusting moment, he licked the plunger before attacking his opponent with it, drawing audible groans from the audience.

The Missing Link's Headbutts and Drool: The Missing Link was known for his wild headbutts and constant drooling, giving him a feral, unhygienic presence in the ring. Fans were equally repelled and fascinated by his savage behavior.

Heidenreich's Poem Recitals: Heidenreich's bizarre habit of reciting unsettling poems while pinning opponents in compromising positions was uncomfortable for everyone involved. His eerie delivery added an extra layer of creepiness to his matches.

Abdullah the Butcher's Bladed Forehead: Years of blading left Abdullah with a deeply scarred forehead that would often bleed profusely during matches. The sight of blood pouring from his head was a shocking and grotesque spectacle for fans.

Chainsaw Charlie and His Sawdust: Terry Funk's Chainsaw Charlie persona involved throwing sawdust into the ring and at his opponents. The gritty mess left wrestlers and fans alike wishing for a cleaner bout.

Goofy Villains:

Characters Rejected by Fans

The Gobbledy Gooker's Infamous Debut: At *Survivor Series 1990*, fans eagerly awaited the unveiling of a mysterious egg, only for the Gobbledy Gooker, a man in a turkey costume, to emerge. Intended as a comedic mascot, the character was met with overwhelming boos and confusion. Despite his brief appearance, the Gooker became synonymous with one of wrestling's biggest missteps.

Heels of the Ring

Shockmaster's Legendary Fall: In WCW, the Shockmaster was hyped as a fearsome new heel, but his debut went awry when he tripped and fell through a wall on live television. Wearing a glitter-covered Stormtrooper helmet, the character quickly became a laughingstock. Fans rejected the gimmick, and Shockmaster's career never recovered.

Repo Man: The Gimmick Nobody Wanted: As a sneaky villain who repossessed property from other wrestlers and fans, Repo Man failed to resonate with audiences. His comical outfit and exaggerated antics made it hard for fans to take him seriously. The character was quickly relegated to mid-card status and became a punchline in wrestling history.

The Red Rooster's Feathered Fiasco: Terry Taylor's transformation into the Red Rooster, complete with a red mohawk and chicken-like strut, was met with derision. Fans struggled to connect with the bizarre gimmick, and Taylor's considerable in-ring talent was overshadowed by the absurdity of the character.

The Yeti's Awkward Hug: During WCW's *Halloween Havoc 1995*, The Yeti emerged wrapped in toilet paper and awkwardly bearhugged Hulk Hogan during a match. Intended as a monstrous threat, the character's clumsy presentation and ridiculous costume turned him into an unintentional comedy act. The Yeti quickly disappeared from WCW programming.

Mantaur's Bovine Blunder: Debuting in WWE in the mid-90s, Mantaur was a wrestler dressed as a half-man, half-bull creature, complete with a large horned headpiece. His gimmick's absurdity and lack of compelling storylines made him an easy target for fan ridicule. Mantaur's brief run in WWE left little impact beyond mockery.

Battle Kat's Puzzling Persona: A masked wrestler with feline-inspired moves, Battle Kat failed to find his footing in WWE. His lack of character depth and connection with fans led to a short-lived run. Despite solid in-ring skills, the gimmick was too silly to succeed.

Duke "The Dumpster" Droese: A Gimmick in the Trash: Portraying a wrestling garbage man, Duke "The Dumpster" Droese failed to capture fan interest. While his work ethic was admirable, the gimmick lacked the depth needed to elevate him beyond mid-card status. Fans quickly dismissed him as another forgettable character of the era.

Oz: A Wizard of a Flop: Before Kevin Nash became a wrestling icon, he portrayed Oz, a character inspired by *The Wizard of Oz*. Complete with a green cape and elaborate entrance, the gimmick was overly theatrical and failed to connect with audiences. Nash's later success highlighted how ill-suited he was for such a cartoonish role.

The Goon: Hockey Meets Wrestling: Dressed in hockey gear and sliding into the ring like he was on ice, The Goon was a wrestler whose gimmick felt more like a parody than a serious competitor. Fans struggled to invest in a character so far removed from traditional wrestling personas.

Beaver Cleavage: A Gimmick Gone Awry: A parody of 1950s sitcoms, Beaver Cleavage debuted in WWE with awkward and suggestive undertones. The character's presentation was widely criticized, and the gimmick was abandoned almost immediately. It remains a prime example of a poorly conceived wrestling persona.

Arachnaman: A Legal Web of Trouble: A blatant Spider-Man knockoff, Arachnaman debuted in WCW in the early 1990s but quickly disappeared due to copyright issues. Fans mocked the character's lack of originality and his overly bright purple-and-yellow costume, making him a short-lived and forgettable villain.

Phantasio: The Magician Wrestler: Phantasio's magic-themed gimmick involved pulling tricks like removing opponents' underwear mid-match. While unique, the character's lack of depth and over-the-top antics didn't resonate with fans. He only appeared in WWE briefly before vanishing from the spotlight.

Shortest Heel Runs:

Villains Who Didn't Last

Stone Cold Steve Austin's Brief Alliance with Vince McMahon: At *WrestleMania X-Seven*, Stone Cold shocked the world by aligning with Vince McMahon to defeat The Rock and win the WWE Championship. However, fans rejected Austin's heel turn, preferring his rebellious antihero persona. Within months, Austin reverted to his more familiar character, making this one of the shortest and most polarizing heel runs in history.

Hulk Hogan's Mr. America Experiment: After years as a beloved face, Hulk Hogan briefly embraced a heel persona as Mr. America in 2003, donning a mask and playing a patriotic antihero. The gimmick was poorly received, and Hogan abandoned the character after just a few months, returning to his classic hero status.

Goldberg's Forced Heel Turn in WCW: In the waning days of WCW, Goldberg was inexplicably turned heel despite his massive popularity as a face. Fans refused to boo the powerhouse, and his heel run lasted only a few weeks before the company reverted him to his original persona. The decision highlighted WCW's creative struggles during its final years.

Trish Stratus' Heel Turn on Chris Jericho: At *WrestleMania XX*, Trish Stratus shocked fans by betraying Chris Jericho and aligning with Christian. Despite the dramatic storyline, her time as a villain was brief, as fans preferred her as a heroic figure in the women's division. Trish returned to being a face within months.

Bret Hart in WCW: After his legendary WWE career, Bret Hart's heel turn in WCW as part of the nWo fell flat due to inconsistent storytelling and fan loyalty to his past persona. The poorly executed angle ended quickly, leaving Hart's WCW run mired in missed opportunities.

Lex Luger's Narcissist Phase: After debuting in WWF as "The Narcissist," Lex Luger's heel persona failed to resonate with fans. The character's arrogance and lack of depth led to a quick rebranding as a patriotic face, culminating in his "All-American" push. His heel run was one of the shortest in WWF history.

Daniel Bryan's Corporate Champion Angle: For a brief period in 2013, Daniel Bryan aligned with The Authority as their chosen champion. Fans rejected this storyline, as Bryan's underdog appeal clashed with the corporate alignment. The angle was scrapped, and Bryan returned to his beloved underdog role.

Villain Turns Rejected by Fans

Hulk Hogan Joins the Dungeon of Doom: While Hulk Hogan's heel turn with the nWo was a massive success, his earlier alignment with the Dungeon of Doom in WCW fell flat. Fans rejected the cartoonish stable and its over-the-top antics, leading to Hogan's quick exit from the group. The storyline highlighted the importance of believable villains in wrestling.

Becky Lynch Turns on Charlotte Flair: During *SummerSlam 2018*, Becky Lynch attacked Charlotte Flair after losing a title match, signaling a heel turn. However, fans cheered Lynch's defiance and rallied behind her transformation into "The Man." WWE quickly pivoted, leaning into Lynch's antihero persona rather than forcing her as a villain.

The Rock's 2003 Hollywood Turn: Upon returning from Hollywood, The Rock attempted a heel turn by mocking fans and his opponents. However, his natural charisma and unmatched mic skills made it impossible for audiences to boo him. His short-lived villainous run ended with fans fully embracing him once again.

Roman Reigns' "Suffering Succotash" Era: Before embracing his Tribal Chief persona, Roman Reigns was pushed as a heel with forced and awkward promos, including the infamous "suffering succotash" line. Fans rejected the unnatural scripting and lack of authenticity, prompting WWE to rethink his character direction.

Daniel Bryan's Eco-Friendly Villainy: While Daniel Bryan's "Planet's Champion" persona was creative, fans struggled to fully buy into his villainous turn given his reputation as an underdog hero. His scathing promos on environmental issues often drew more confusion than heat, leading to a mixed reaction from audiences.

Seth Rollins as The Messiah: Seth Rollins' "Monday Night Messiah" character aimed to create a cult-like heel persona, but the over-the-top promos and convoluted storylines left fans divided. While the character had moments of brilliance, it ultimately struggled to sustain consistent heat, leading to Rollins shifting focus.

CM Punk Aligns with Paul Heyman: CM Punk's alignment with Paul Heyman after his WWE title reign initially seemed like a strong heel move. However, fans' respect for Punk's charisma and skill made it hard to fully hate him. The partnership ended abruptly, with Punk transitioning back to a more balanced character.

Kurt Angle's "You Suck" Era: While Kurt Angle's early heel antics were meant to draw heat, his comedic timing and athleticism won fans over. Chants of "You Suck" became endearing rather than insulting, turning his villainous run into an unintentionally beloved phase of his career.

Randy Orton Joins The Authority: Randy Orton's alignment with The Authority was designed to make him the face of WWE's corporate machine. However, fans saw Orton as more effective as a lone predator, and the storyline struggled to connect. Orton's eventual turn against The Authority highlighted his natural antihero appeal.

Weapons of Destruction

In professional wrestling, villains are masters of bending the rules, but some heels take their treachery to another level with the weapons of destruction they wield. These tools, both literal and psychological, become extensions of their villainy, elevating them from ordinary rule-breakers to legends of mayhem. Whether it's a steel chair wielded in the heat of battle or the searing words of psychological warfare, these "weapons" make wrestling's heels unforgettable.

Wrestling rings may have ropes and rules, but for heels, those are merely suggestions. They thrive on chaos, and their ingenuity in finding ways to gain an advantage knows no bounds. Some rely on tangible props—like Triple H's sledgehammer or Abdullah the Butcher's infamous fork—to make their mark. Others lean into the theater of wrestling, using their minds as their greatest weapon to unsettle opponents and audiences alike. And then there are those who take the fight outside the ring entirely, turning vehicles and everyday objects into tools of destruction.

The beauty of these weapons lies in their versatility. Chairs, chains, and brass knuckles are just the beginning. Hardcore legends push the envelope with barbed wire, flaming tables, and even thumbtacks. But not all weapons are physical—villains like Bray Wyatt have shown that fear and mind games can be as debilitating as any foreign object. The psychology of wrestling's villains often lingers longer than their matches, leaving scars that extend beyond the physical.

This section dives into the many ways villains weaponize the world around them to solidify their dominance. You'll read about the signature props that became synonymous with their names, from The Mountie's cattle prod to The Great Kabuki's green mist. You'll revisit the carnage of hardcore wrestling and the moments that pushed fans to their limits. And you'll see how vehicles—from ambulances to limousines—turned into tools of destruction, making headlines for their shocking spectacle.

Villains in wrestling are more than just bad guys—they're innovators of chaos, finding ways to disrupt the status quo and leave a lasting impression. Whether they're wielding a sledgehammer, setting up a flaming table, or getting into their opponent's head with haunting words, these weapons of destruction define their legacy. So buckle up—things are about to get dangerous.

Signature Weapons and Props:

Tools of the Villains

Triple H's Sledgehammer: Triple H's sledgehammer became a symbol of his dominance and ruthlessness throughout his career. Whether smashing it into the ribs of his opponents or using it as a psychological prop, it became synonymous with his calculated, cerebral style. Most notably, he used the sledgehammer to dismantle legends like The Undertaker during their battles at *WrestleMania*.

The Mountie's Cattle Prod: As one of the most devious heels of the early 1990s, The Mountie carried a cattle prod he dubbed the "Shock Stick." He often waited until the referee's back was turned to zap his opponents, leaving them incapacitated. One of his most infamous uses of the cattle prod was during his Intercontinental Championship victory over Bret Hart, a match that cemented his villainous reputation.

Mick Foley's Barbed-Wire Bat: Wrestling as Cactus Jack, Mick Foley's barbed-wire bat was a hallmark of his hardcore matches. This gruesome weapon was not just for show—Foley swung it with reckless abandon, often cutting himself and his opponents in the process. In a brutal feud with Terry Funk, Foley's barbed-wire bat was central to the chaos, leading to some of the bloodiest matches in wrestling history.

Kendo Sticks in Hardcore Matches: The kendo stick became a signature weapon of ECW legends like The Sandman and Tommy Dreamer. These wooden canes weren't just for show—they left welts and bruises on anyone unlucky enough to be struck. One of the most iconic uses of a kendo stick occurred during The Sandman's feud with Raven, where the stick's brutal sound echoed through the arena as fans cheered for the carnage.

The Great Kabuki's Green Mist: The Great Kabuki brought the art of spitting green mist to disorient and blind his opponents. This tactic, often used during high-stakes matches, gave Kabuki an undeniable advantage. A memorable moment came during a match in Japan where he blinded Dusty Rhodes, turning the tide in an otherwise even contest. This tactic was later popularized by Tajiri, keeping the tradition alive.

Brass Knuckles: William Regal's Hidden Edge: William Regal's brass knuckles were as sneaky as his villainous grin. Hidden in his tights, the knuckles would appear at crucial moments, allowing Regal to knock out his unsuspecting opponents. A defining moment came during his feud with Edge, where a single blow with the knuckles turned a grueling match into a quick victory for the cunning villain.

Jake "The Snake" Roberts and Damien: Jake Roberts' python, Damien, wasn't just a gimmick, but a weapon of terror. In one of his most memorable moments, Roberts unleashed Damien on Andre the Giant during their feud, exploiting Andre's well-known fear of snakes. Andre, visibly panicked, stumbled and even appeared to have a heart attack in the ring, adding to the drama. This chilling use of Damien intensified their rivalry and showcased Roberts' ability to blend psychological warfare with in-ring storytelling.

Abdullah the Butcher's Fork: Abdullah the Butcher's fork was a gruesome addition to his arsenal, used to carve into the foreheads of his opponents. His matches with Bruiser Brody became infamous for their sheer brutality, with blood flowing freely as Abdullah wielded the fork with no restraint. Fans were both horrified and mesmerized by his willingness to push boundaries.

Eddie Guerrero's Steel Chair Deception: Eddie Guerrero turned the steel chair into a tool of comedic villainy by often pretending to be struck and tossing the chair to his opponent while the referee looked on. One particularly memorable use of this tactic came during a match against Kurt Angle, where Guerrero's antics led to Angle's disqualification, much to the crowd's delight.

Heels of the Ring

Big Boss Man's Nightstick: As part of his law enforcement gimmick, Big Boss Man's nightstick was both a symbol of authority and a tool of oppression. In his feuds with Hulk Hogan and The Big Show, the nightstick played a pivotal role in his dirty tactics, leaving opponents battered and humiliated.

Honky Tonk Man's Guitar Smashes: The Honky Tonk Man's guitar became a weapon of choice, often smashing it over his opponents' heads. One of the most famous instances involved Jake Roberts, whose storyline injuries from a guitar shot sparked a heated rivalry that captivated fans.

Terry Funk's Branding Iron: Terry Funk's branding iron wasn't just a cowboy prop—it was a weapon that embodied his unrelenting style. During his matches in WCW and ECW, Funk used the branding iron to burn his opponents, adding a literal and symbolic mark of his dominance.

Al Snow and Head: Al Snow's mannequin head, simply called "Head," became an unusual but iconic weapon. He often brought Head to the ring as both a companion and a blunt object, using it to knock out opponents. During his time in ECW and WWF, Snow's bizarre antics, combined with Head's unpredictability, added a surreal and comedic element to his matches.

Steve Blackman and His Kendo Sticks: Known as "The Lethal Weapon," Steve Blackman often wielded kendo sticks with precision and brutality. His martial arts background made his use of the sticks particularly devastating, with memorable moments including his hardcore matches against Shane McMahon, where the weapon was central to the action.

Fit Finlay and the Shillelagh: Fit Finlay's shillelagh was a nod to his Irish heritage, but it was also a deadly weapon in the ring. Finlay used the sturdy club to attack opponents, often targeting their legs or backs to weaken them. This weapon played a pivotal role in his feuds on SmackDown, cementing his reputation as a crafty and relentless competitor.

The Undertaker and the Urn: The Undertaker's mystical urn, carried by his manager Paul Bearer, symbolized his supernatural powers. Heels would often target the urn to disrupt The Undertaker's focus, leading to dramatic moments where the urn became a weapon itself. One iconic instance saw Bearer striking The Undertaker with the urn, shocking fans and turning the tide of a major match.

Rick "The Model" Martel and His Arrogance Spray: Rick Martel's cologne bottle, dubbed "Arrogance," was more than just a vanity prop—it was a weapon. Martel often sprayed the substance into his opponents' eyes, temporarily blinding them and securing cheap victories. This tactic became central to his heel persona and his feuds with stars like Jake Roberts.

When Villains Went Too Far:

Real Injuries Caused by Heels

Bruiser Brody and Jose Gonzalez: In one of wrestling's darkest moments, Bruiser Brody was fatally stabbed by fellow wrestler Jose Gonzalez backstage before a match in Puerto Rico. Brody's injuries were so severe that he died in the hospital shortly after. The shocking incident stunned the wrestling world and highlighted a lack of proper security and oversight in certain promotions.

Sid Vicious vs. Brian Pillman: During a WCW match, Sid Vicious delivered a powerbomb to Brian Pillman that was executed improperly, leaving Pillman with a legitimate shoulder injury. Pillman required weeks of recovery, and the botched move became an infamous example of how miscommunication in the ring could result in real harm.

Vader's Eye Incident: During a match in Japan against Stan Hansen, Vader's eye popped out of its socket after a stiff punch. Despite the severity of the injury, Vader pushed his eye back in and continued the match. He later required surgery to address the damage, and the incident cemented his reputation as one of wrestling's toughest competitors.

The Great Khali's Botched Chop: In a training session, The Great Khali delivered a powerful chop to another wrestler's head, causing severe trauma that required immediate medical attention. The injured wrestler was hospitalized, raising concerns about the risks posed by oversized competitors using uncontrolled moves.

Shawn Michaels and Owen Hart's Enziguri: Owen Hart's enziguri kick to Shawn Michaels during a match caused a legitimate concussion, forcing Michaels to take months off from in-ring competition. This extended absence underscored the dangers of head injuries in wrestling, even from routine moves.

Brock Lesnar's Shooting Star Press: At *WrestleMania XIX*, Brock Lesnar attempted a shooting star press on Kurt Angle but landed awkwardly on his head. Lesnar suffered a concussion and a strained neck but miraculously finished the match. He later required medical evaluation, though he avoided surgery.

New Jack and Mass Transit: During an ECW event, New Jack used a blade on a young, inexperienced wrestler named Mass Transit, causing excessive bleeding. The wrestler required immediate medical attention and stitches, and the incident led to a lawsuit against ECW. The controversy tarnished New Jack's reputation further.

Mick Foley and The Rock's Chair Shots: At *Royal Rumble 1999*, The Rock delivered multiple unprotected chair shots to Mick Foley's head while his hands were tied behind his back. Foley suffered a severe concussion and required time off to recover. The incident sparked conversations about wrestler safety and the dangers of head trauma.

Sabu and Terry Funk's Barbed Wire Match: During a gruesome barbed wire match, Sabu legitimately tore his bicep on the wire and had to tape it mid-match to continue. He later required over 100 stitches, and the incident showcased the extreme lengths hardcore wrestlers were willing to go for their craft.

Hulk Hogan vs. Antonio Inoki: During a match in Japan, Hulk Hogan's botched clothesline left Antonio Inoki unconscious. Inoki required medical attention but recovered quickly. The incident raised concerns about stiff moves and the potential for serious harm in the ring.

Goldberg vs. Bret Hart: Goldberg's botched kick to Bret Hart's head during a WCW match caused a severe concussion that ultimately ended Hart's career. Hart required months of recovery, but lingering symptoms forced him into early retirement.

Randy Orton and The Singh Brothers: During a match on *SmackDown*, Randy Orton slammed one of The Singh Brothers onto the announce table with excessive force, causing a legitimate back injury. The injured Singh Brother required physical therapy but returned to action after a short hiatus.

Big Van Vader's Nose Break: In a match against Cactus Jack, Vader broke Jack's nose with a stiff forearm. Jack's nose required resetting and time off to heal, though he later praised Vader for the intensity he brought to their matches.

Triple H's Sledgehammer on Daniel Bryan: Triple H's use of a sledgehammer during a match with Daniel Bryan led to a legitimate chest injury, sidelining Bryan for several weeks. The visual appeal of the weapon often masked its potential for real harm.

Andre the Giant's Stiff Headbutts: Andre's massive size made his headbutts devastating, and in one match, an overly stiff headbutt left his opponent concussed. The injured wrestler missed a month of action due to lingering symptoms.

CM Punk vs. Ryback: CM Punk publicly criticized Ryback for being reckless in the ring after sustaining multiple injuries during their matches. Punk cited a rib injury and a strained back as examples of Ryback's unsafe practices, which required weeks of recovery.

Seth Rollins and Sting's Buckle Bomb: During a match at *Night of Champions 2015*, Seth Rollins delivered a buckle bomb to Sting that caused severe neck injuries. Sting required extensive medical evaluation and was forced into retirement following the incident.

Yokozuna's Banzai Drop: Yokozuna's massive size made his Banzai Drop a spectacle, but during one match, he landed awkwardly on his opponent, causing a rib injury. The opponent required weeks of rest and recovery before returning to the ring.

The Dudley Boyz and Mae Young: During an infamous moment, The Dudley Boyz powerbombed Mae Young through a table. While the segment was scripted, Mae suffered minor bruises despite her advanced age. Her willingness to take the bump drew both praise and concern.

Rikishi's Stinkface Gone Wrong: During a house show, Rikishi's signature Stinkface move accidentally injured his opponent, who hit their head on the turnbuckle. The opponent required stitches but was able to return to action shortly after.

Jack Swagger's Gutwrench Powerbomb: Swagger's finisher left an opponent with a dislocated shoulder during a live event. The injury required the wrestler to undergo physical therapy and miss several weeks of competition.

Heels of the Ring

Brock Lesnar vs. Randy Orton: At *SummerSlam 2016*, Lesnar delivered legitimate elbow strikes to Orton's head, causing a severe cut that required staples to close. Orton was evaluated for a concussion but returned to action within weeks.

Randy Savage vs. Ricky Steamboat: During their legendary feud, Savage's use of the ring bell in a scripted attack left Steamboat with a real throat injury. Steamboat required weeks to recover, adding intensity to their eventual *WrestleMania III* match.

Steve Austin vs. Owen Hart's Piledriver: Owen Hart delivered a botched piledriver to Steve Austin at *SummerSlam 1997*, resulting in a neck injury that nearly ended Austin's career. Austin was sidelined for months and had lingering neck issues for the rest of his career.

Psychological Weapons:

Mind Games Before the Fight

The Undertaker's Coffin Stunts: The Undertaker would frequently use coffins to intimidate his rivals before major matches. One notable instance involved sending a custom-made casket to Yokozuna ahead of their casket match, amplifying the psychological tension and forcing Yokozuna to confront his own fears before stepping into the ring.

Heels of the Ring

Bray Wyatt's Firefly Fun House: Wyatt's eerie vignettes featured unsettling imagery and cryptic messages, designed to confuse and frighten his opponents. Before his match with John Cena at *WrestleMania 36*, Wyatt used the Fun House segments to mock Cena's career and portray him as a corporate puppet, leaving Cena visibly off his game.

Goldust's Androgynous Persona: Goldust's flamboyant and provocative behavior was meant to unnerve opponents. His psychological warfare shone during his feud with Razor Ramon, where his suggestive advances caused discomfort and distraction in and out of the ring, leaving Ramon visibly disturbed and unable to focus.

Edge's Seduction of Lita: Edge's real-life relationship with Lita was turned into a storyline to torment Matt Hardy. By flaunting their affair on-screen, Edge created an emotionally charged rivalry that blurred the lines between fiction and reality, pushing Hardy to lash out in frustration.

Mankind's Boiler Room Videos: Mankind's eerie vignettes, filmed in boiler rooms, showcased his unsettling demeanor and psychological instability. These segments, filled with cryptic dialogue and unnerving visuals, made opponents wary of facing him in the ring, fearing his unpredictability.

Raven's Cryptic Monologues: Raven often delivered philosophical, melancholic promos that delved into his personal struggles, using them as a way to unsettle opponents. His feud with Tommy Dreamer was laced with mind games that included personal and emotional attacks, leaving Dreamer questioning his own resilience.

The Fiend's Lantern Entrance: Bray Wyatt's Fiend character would carry a lantern shaped like his previous persona's severed head, a visual meant to unsettle both his opponents and the audience. This grotesque symbol of his transformation added psychological weight to his matches, leaving rivals visibly unnerved.

The Big Boss Man's Feud with Big Show: Boss Man took psychological warfare to a new and deeply personal level during his feud with Big Show. Not only did he mock Big Show's late father, but he also interrupted the funeral by arriving in a police car, attaching the casket to the car, and driving off with it in front of a horrified Big Show and his family. The despicable act left Big Show emotionally devastated, and the storyline became one of the most memorable examples of a villain crossing the line in professional wrestling history.

Al Snow and Head's Unnerving Presence: Al Snow's constant conversations with his mannequin head, "Head," unsettled opponents and blurred the line between sanity and madness. The gimmick gave him a psychological advantage by making opponents question his unpredictability and mental state.

Vehicular Villainy: Destruction on Wheels

Stone Cold Steve Austin's Zamboni Attack: During an episode of *Raw is War* in 1998, Stone Cold Steve Austin drove a Zamboni into the arena and rammed it into the ring to confront Vince McMahon. Austin climbed on top of the Zamboni and leapt into the ring, delivering a flurry of punches to McMahon. This iconic moment disrupted McMahon's planned speech and left the crowd roaring in approval, solidifying Austin's status as the ultimate anti-hero who would stop at nothing to defy authority.

The nWo's Monster Truck Battle: At *Halloween Havoc 1995*, Hulk Hogan and The Giant participated in a bizarre monster truck sumo match atop a building. The match ended with The Giant falling off the roof, only to reappear later in the night to continue their feud. The event bewildered fans, and the dramatic "fall" symbolized the nWo's over-the-top storytelling that blurred the line between reality and fiction.

Eddie Guerrero's Lowrider Exploits: Eddie Guerrero's lowrider wasn't just a prop; it became an extension of his character. During his feud with JBL, Eddie used his lowrider to intimidate his opponent, even pretending to run over JBL during a heated segment. This act of mock aggression elevated their rivalry, showcasing Guerrero's ability to balance humor and intensity while keeping fans thoroughly entertained.

Big Show Flipping a Jeep: During a backstage segment, Big Show displayed his immense strength by flipping a jeep belonging to his rival, Brock Lesnar. This act of vehicular destruction was designed to intimidate Lesnar and showcased Big Show's monstrous persona. The feat left commentators and fans alike in awe, emphasizing the sheer power of wrestling's larger-than-life characters.

Brock Lesnar's Forklift Ambush: During a feud with Roman Reigns, Brock Lesnar used a forklift to lift and topple Reigns' car. This dramatic display of destruction left Reigns shaken and forced him to rethink his strategy. The segment showcased Lesnar's unpredictable nature and added a visceral edge to their rivalry.

Goldberg's Car Smashing: Goldberg was famous for smashing cars as part of his entrance during his WCW days. In one memorable moment, he destroyed a limousine with his bare hands and a steel pipe, showcasing his ferocity and brute strength. The visual of Goldberg surrounded by shattered glass became a lasting image of his unstoppable persona.

Vince McMahon's Limo Explosion: In a controversial storyline, Vince McMahon's limousine was rigged to explode during a *Raw* broadcast. Though fictional, the dramatic visual shocked fans and briefly hinted at McMahon's "death" in the storyline. The segment was later scrapped due to real-world events, but it remains a shocking example of vehicular drama.

Shawn Michaels' DX Tank Entrance: As part of a legendary DX invasion of WCW, Shawn Michaels and Triple H arrived in a tank-like vehicle. Though the invasion was tongue-in-cheek, it symbolized the rebellious nature of DX and their willingness to take the fight to their competitors. The segment became a defining moment of the Monday Night Wars.

The Dudley Boyz and the Car Crash: During an ECW storyline, The Dudley Boyz orchestrated a staged car crash involving their opponents. The shocking angle pushed the boundaries of storytelling and left fans questioning its realism. It showcased the extreme lengths ECW would go to captivate its audience.

Austin's Cement Truck Prank: Stone Cold Steve Austin famously filled Vince McMahon's Corvette with cement during a live segment on *Raw*. The act of destruction was a perfect representation of Austin's anti-authority persona and remains one of the most memorable vehicular moments in wrestling history. The visual of cement overflowing from the car became an iconic symbol of Austin's rebellion.

Rikishi's Hit-and-Run on Stone Cold: In a storyline that shocked fans, it was revealed that Rikishi had hit Stone Cold Steve Austin with a car, putting Austin out of action for months. The revelation added a layer of mystery and betrayal to the feud, with Rikishi claiming he "did it for The Rock," further fueling tensions between the characters.

Carnage in Hardcore Wrestling

Terry Funk and Mick Foley's Barbed Wire Match: Terry Funk and Mick Foley (as Cactus Jack) faced off in a barbed wire match in Japan that pushed the limits of brutality. Both wrestlers were tangled in barbed wire multiple times, with Foley suffering deep cuts across his arms and back. The match became a defining moment for hardcore wrestling, showcasing the sheer physical toll it demanded.

ECW's Massacre on Queens Boulevard: At this event, The Sandman and Tommy Dreamer clashed in a brutal Singapore cane match. Dreamer's back was left raw and bleeding after repeated strikes from The Sandman, while the crowd chanted for more. This match cemented ECW's reputation for embracing blood and violence as key storytelling elements.

The Original Hell in a Cell Match: In 1997, Shawn Michaels and The Undertaker battled in the first-ever Hell in a Cell match. The bout included high-impact moves using the steel structure, with Michaels suffering a brutal fall off the side of the cage through an announce table. The match set the standard for hardcore action in WWE's main events.

The Taipei Deathmatch: Ian Rotten and Axl Rotten faced off in one of the most infamous hardcore wrestling matches ever, where both men taped shards of broken glass to their fists. Each blow left deep cuts, with the ring stained in blood by the end of the match. This grotesque spectacle horrified some fans but became legendary within hardcore wrestling circles.

The Flaming Table Spot: The Dudley Boyz popularized flaming table spots, most notably during their ECW days. In one match, they powerbombed Spike Dudley through a table set ablaze, leaving the crowd in shock. The visual of the flames combined with Spike's brutal landing encapsulated the extreme nature of hardcore wrestling.

New Jack's Balcony Dive: New Jack was infamous for his high-risk dives, including a shocking leap off a 20-foot balcony onto Vic Grimes in XPW. Both men suffered injuries, with Grimes reportedly breaking his ankle on impact. This reckless moment showcased New Jack's penchant for pushing the limits of safety.

Mick Foley's Fall Through the Cell: At *King of the Ring 1998*, Mick Foley was thrown off the top of the Hell in a Cell by The Undertaker, landing on the announce table below. Later in the match, he was chokeslammed through the cage roof, crashing into the ring. Foley suffered a dislocated shoulder, missing teeth, and a concussion, but the match solidified his legacy as the ultimate hardcore icon.

The Exploding Barbed Wire Deathmatch: In FMW, Atsushi Onita and Terry Funk competed in an Exploding Barbed Wire Deathmatch, where the ropes were replaced with barbed wire rigged to explode on contact. Both men suffered burns and lacerations, with the match ending in a dramatic explosion that left the crowd stunned. This became one of the most infamous matches in hardcore history.

CZW's Tournament of Death: Combat Zone Wrestling's annual Tournament of Death features some of the most violent matches in wrestling. One match saw Nick Gage suffer a deep wound from light tubes, requiring emergency medical attention. The tournament's notoriety comes from its sheer brutality, drawing hardcore fans from around the world.

Tommy Dreamer's Cheese Grater Spot: Dreamer's feud with Raven included a gruesome moment where Raven raked a cheese grater across Dreamer's forehead. The blood flowed freely, and the visual became one of the most iconic in ECW's history. This spot exemplified the lengths hardcore wrestlers would go to for storytelling.

Terry Funk's Flaming Branding Iron: Terry Funk introduced a flaming branding iron into one of his matches in Japan, using it to strike his opponent and ignite parts of the ring. The spectacle caused panic among fans and officials, solidifying Funk's reputation as a master of hardcore chaos.

Jon Moxley's Lights Out Match: Before joining AEW, Jon Moxley (formerly Dean Ambrose) competed in a Lights Out Match with Kenny Omega that involved barbed wire, broken glass, and mousetraps. Both men left the match bloodied, with Moxley's defiant persona cemented as a modern hardcore legend.

Darby Allin's Thumbtack Skateboard: In AEW, Darby Allin introduced a skateboard with thumbtacks attached to the underside. He used it to grind across his opponent's back, leaving visible punctures and adding a new dimension to hardcore innovation.

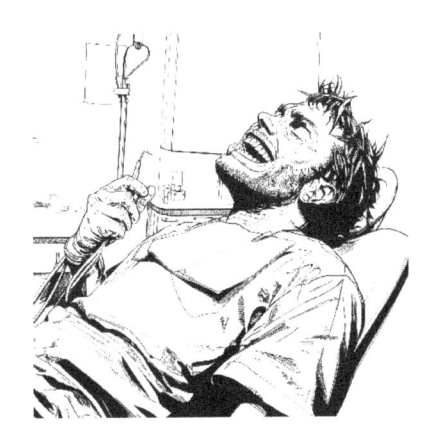

Early Characters of Notorious Wrestling Villains

The Undertaker as Mean Mark Callous: Before donning the hat and trench coat, The Undertaker wrestled in WCW as Mean Mark Callous, a red-haired powerhouse. Though talented, the character didn't stand out until his transformation into the Deadman. This shift turned him into one of wrestling's most iconic figures.

Triple H as Hunter Hearst Helmsley: Triple H began his WWE career as a snobbish aristocrat who emphasized his wealth and refined demeanor. While the character gained attention, it wasn't until he joined D-Generation X and embraced a rebellious attitude that he truly found his stride.

Kane as Isaac Yankem, DDS: Before becoming the Big Red Machine, Kane played Isaac Yankem, an evil dentist allied with Jerry Lawler. The character was widely panned, leading to Kane's eventual reinvention as The Undertaker's demonic brother. The dramatic shift brought him lasting success.

Chris Jericho as Lionheart: In his early days in WCW, Chris Jericho wrestled under the moniker Lionheart, portraying a clean-cut, high-flying babyface. While talented, the character lacked the charisma that Jericho later displayed as a villain in WWE.

Becky Lynch as "The Irish Lass Kicker": Before becoming "The Man," Becky Lynch was a plucky underdog who leaned into her Irish heritage. Her early babyface persona lacked the edge that later defined her as a villain-turned-anti-hero. The transformation elevated her to superstardom.

Edge as Sexton Hardcastle: Before his Rated-R Superstar days, Edge wrestled on the independent scene as Sexton Hardcastle, a flamboyant and comical character. This early persona was worlds apart from the edgy, manipulative villain he became in WWE.

Ric Flair as a Babyface Rookie: In his early career, Ric Flair was a clean-cut babyface in the AWA, far removed from the arrogant "Nature Boy" persona. His eventual embrace of flashy robes, arrogance, and catchphrases made him one of wrestling's most iconic heels.

Kevin Nash as Oz in WCW: Long before becoming Diesel or Big Sexy, Kevin Nash portrayed Oz, a gimmick inspired by *The Wizard of Oz*. The character flopped, leading to Nash's reinvention as one of the coolest villains of the nWo era.

Jobber Villains:

The Stars Who Rarely Won

The Brooklyn Brawler: Steve Lombardi, better known as The Brooklyn Brawler, became one of WWE's most famous jobbers. His gritty New York persona, complete with a torn shirt and brawler attitude, made him a perfect foil for rising stars. Brawler would often taunt the audience and opponents, establishing himself as a scrappy villain who embraced his role as a perpetual underdog, even as he lost.

Heels of the Ring

Barry Horowitz: Known for patting himself on the back after matches, Barry Horowitz's self-aggrandizing antics often amused fans. His overconfidence and smug attitude turned him into a subtle villain, always celebrating prematurely before inevitably losing. When he shockingly defeated Skip of the Bodydonnas, it was a rare moment where the crowd rallied behind a jobber who had made them boo moments before.

Iron Mike Sharpe: Dubbed "Canada's Greatest Athlete," Iron Mike Sharpe's constant boasting and use of his black forearm brace as an illegal weapon added a layer of villainy to his otherwise consistent losing streak. Sharpe's loud grunts and exaggerated reactions in the ring made him a memorable character who relished in bending the rules, even if it rarely worked in his favor.

Johnny Rodz: As a WWE Hall of Famer, Johnny Rodz was a respected jobber who wrestled throughout the 1970s and 1980s. His scrappy style and occasional dirty tactics, such as choking opponents on the ropes, made him an effective villain in his era. Rodz's ability to convincingly antagonize his opponents ensured he played a key role in elevating rising stars.

Heels of the Ring

George South: A staple of Jim Crockett Promotions, George South often played the arrogant loser who underestimated his opponents. South's knack for mocking the crowd and taunting his rivals added a layer of antagonism to his matches. Even in defeat, his ability to sell moves convincingly made every bout feel significant.

The Mulkey Brothers: Randy and Bill Mulkey became infamous for their consistent losing streak in WCW, often playing cowardly and bumbling villains. Their rare victory against The Gladiators, dubbed "The Mulkey Miracle," was celebrated by fans who enjoyed their underdog charm. Despite their comedic style, the Mulkey Brothers excelled at making their opponents look dominant.

The Gambler: A frequent jobber in WCW, The Gambler's casino-themed gimmick included flashy card-patterned gear and a cocky attitude. Though rarely victorious, his character relied on arrogance and showmanship to entertain the audience. The Gambler became a memorable villain in the enhancement talent roster by feigning confidence.

S.D. Jones: Special Delivery Jones gained fame for his energetic entrances and quick losses. His most infamous moment came at *WrestleMania I*, where he lost to King Kong Bundy in just nine seconds. Jones often played the role of the overconfident underdog, taunting opponents before his inevitable defeat, which endeared him to fans.

Barry O: Part of the famous Orton wrestling family, Barry O often played the arrogant heel who believed his lineage made him unbeatable. This overconfidence made his frequent losses even more satisfying for fans. His consistent dedication to the role ensured he was a reliable foil for rising stars.

Rene Goulet: A veteran of WWE's early days, Rene Goulet often found himself on the losing end of matches against rising stars. His flamboyant ring gear and theatrical style added a layer of arrogance to his persona, making his defeats feel like just desserts for his villainy. Goulet's exaggerated reactions helped elevate his opponents.

Tiger Chung Lee: Known for his menacing persona, Tiger Chung Lee was a fixture in WWE during the 1980s. His intimidating look and occasional use of illegal moves, like choking opponents, added to his aura as a villain. Despite his losing record, his unique style and presence left a lasting impression on fans.

Wrestling Announcers Who Supported Villains

Bobby "The Brain" Heenan: Bobby Heenan was the quintessential villainous announcer, openly rooting for heels while belittling fan favorites. His quick wit and sarcastic commentary added a layer of humor to matches, especially when he defended Ric Flair or Mr. Perfect. When Ric Flair won the 1992 Royal Rumble, Heenan exclaimed, "Yes! Yes! Yes! The real world champion has done it!" cementing his unwavering support for the Nature Boy.

Jesse "The Body" Ventura: As a color commentator, Jesse Ventura consistently sided with the bad guys, often praising their cunning and strategy. His defense of rule-breaking tactics, such as using foreign objects, made him a foil to play-by-play announcers like Gorilla Monsoon. When cheering on Rick Rude, Ventura famously quipped, "That's not cheating, Monsoon, that's using your head!"

Paul Heyman: During his time as a commentator in WCW and later in ECW, Paul Heyman (as Paul E. Dangerously) championed heel wrestlers with sharp, biting analysis. His ability to justify the actions of villains, such as The Dangerous Alliance, showcased his intellect and bias. When defending his faction's underhanded tactics, Heyman once declared, "It's not illegal if you don't get caught."

Jerry "The King" Lawler: Jerry Lawler frequently sided with villains during his time as a WWE commentator, often mocking the good guys and cheering for underhanded tactics. His relentless taunting of Bret Hart during their feud added a personal edge to his commentary. When Bret Hart was attacked by Yokozuna, Lawler gleefully exclaimed, "That's what he deserves! Hit him harder, Yokozuna!"

Corey Graves; Corey Graves' modern take on villainous commentary includes consistently siding with wrestlers like Baron Corbin and Roman Reigns during their heel runs. Graves often delivers sarcastic quips and defends the villains' actions with a smug confidence. During Roman Reigns' brutal attack on Kevin Owens, Graves shouted, "This is dominance! Reigns is showing everyone why he's the Head of the Table!"

Michael Cole (Corporate Phase): During his alignment with The Miz and the anonymous Raw General Manager, Michael Cole adopted a heel commentator persona. He frequently criticized fan favorites like Daniel Bryan while championing The Miz as WWE Champion. Cole once proclaimed, "The Miz is the hero we need—he's showing everyone what true greatness looks like!"

Jim Cornette: During his commentary stints, Jim Cornette often praised heels for their cunning and strategy while berating faces for being naïve. His knowledge of wrestling history allowed him to justify villainous actions as part of the sport's tradition. When defending Yokozuna's use of salt against Bret Hart, Cornette remarked, "That's not cheating, that's tradition from the sumo world!"

Heel JR (WWE's Experiment): During a brief stint as a heel commentator, Jim Ross aligned himself with Dr. Death Steve Williams and adopted a more arrogant persona. While short-lived, this experiment showcased Ross's versatility and added an intriguing dynamic to WWE broadcasts. Ross once stated, "Dr. Death doesn't just beat opponents; he obliterates them!"

Pat McAfee: While not exclusively a heel, Pat McAfee's commentary often includes enthusiastic praise for wrestlers like Roman Reigns and The Usos during their villainous phases. His larger-than-life personality and willingness to bend the narrative make him a standout voice. During a Roman Reigns promo, McAfee excitedly said, "The Tribal Chief is showing the world why this is his island!"

Celebrity Showdowns with Villains

Mr. T vs. Roddy Piper: At *WrestleMania I*, Mr. T teamed with Hulk Hogan to face Roddy Piper and Paul Orndorff in the main event. Piper's villainous antics included mocking Mr. T's acting career and taunting him in promos. During the match, Mr. T held his own, delivering body slams and punches, solidifying his place in wrestling history.

Mike Tyson Aligns with DX: In 1998, Mike Tyson served as the special enforcer for the main event of *WrestleMania XIV* between Stone Cold Steve Austin and Shawn Michaels. Although initially aligned with Michaels and DX, Tyson shocked everyone by siding with Austin, delivering a knockout punch to Michaels after the match. This moment cemented Tyson's crossover appeal and added drama to Austin's rise.

Cyndi Lauper vs. The Fabulous Moolah: During the "Rock 'n' Wrestling" era, Cyndi Lauper managed Wendi Richter in her feud against The Fabulous Moolah. Lauper played an active role in ringside antics, even hitting Moolah with her purse during a pivotal match. Her involvement brought mainstream attention to women's wrestling.

Arnold Schwarzenegger vs. Triple H: On an episode of *SmackDown*, Arnold Schwarzenegger confronted Triple H during a promo. The interaction escalated into a physical altercation, with Schwarzenegger landing a punch that sent Triple H reeling. The crowd erupted as Arnold's real-life action hero persona translated seamlessly into the wrestling ring.

Floyd Mayweather vs. Big Show: At *WrestleMania XXIV*, Floyd "Money" Mayweather faced off against Big Show in a No Disqualification match. Mayweather used his speed and brass knuckles to defeat the larger opponent, breaking Big Show's nose during their buildup. The match highlighted Mayweather's agility and cunning against a towering villain.

Shaquille O'Neal vs. The Big Show: Shaquille O'Neal made an appearance at *WrestleMania 32* during the Andre the Giant Memorial Battle Royal. He squared off with Big Show, engaging in a dramatic face-off that delighted fans. Although their interaction was brief, Shaq's charisma added excitement to the match.

Stephen Amell's Feuds with Stardust and Cody Rhodes: Actor Stephen Amell stepped into the ring at *SummerSlam 2015* to team with Neville against Stardust and King Barrett. Amell surprised fans with his athleticism, executing a crossbody from the top rope to the outside. Later, Amell and Cody Rhodes continued their feud in independent wrestling promotions, where Amell delivered a top-rope dive onto Rhodes, earning respect for his commitment. The rivalry blurred the lines between celebrity and wrestler, showcasing Amell's dedication to the craft.

Jon Stewart vs. Seth Rollins: At *SummerSlam 2015*, Jon Stewart shocked fans by interfering in Seth Rollins' match against John Cena. Stewart used a steel chair to hit Cena, helping Rollins retain his WWE Championship. The comedic twist added a surprising layer to the storyline.

Bad Bunny vs. The Miz: At *WrestleMania 37*, Grammy-winning artist Bad Bunny teamed with Damian Priest to face The Miz and John Morrison. Bunny impressed fans with his dedication, executing moves like a Canadian Destroyer and a crossbody to the outside. His performance elevated the celebrity involvement standard in wrestling.

Donald Trump vs. Vince McMahon: In the "Battle of the Billionaires" at *WrestleMania 23*, Donald Trump managed Bobby Lashley against Vince McMahon's Umaga. After Lashley won, Trump helped shave McMahon's head, delivering one of the most iconic celebrity moments in WWE history. The segment brought mainstream media attention to the event.

Machine Gun Kelly vs. Kevin Owens: During a musical performance on *Raw*, Machine Gun Kelly was powerbombed off the stage by Kevin Owens. The dramatic moment was a highlight of the show, with Owens solidifying his heel persona. Kelly's willingness to take the bump earned him respect from wrestling fans.

Logan Paul vs. The Miz: Logan Paul made his WWE debut at *WrestleMania 38*, teaming with The Miz against Rey and Dominik Mysterio. Paul surprised fans with his athleticism, hitting a Frog Splash and other high-flying moves. After the match, The Miz turned on Paul, setting up a future feud.

Muhammad Ali vs. Gorilla Monsoon: During a special segment in 1976, boxing legend Muhammad Ali faced off with Gorilla Monsoon in an exhibition. Monsoon used an airplane spin to disorient Ali, showcasing wrestling's blend of athleticism and theatrics. The encounter demonstrated Ali's respect for the wrestling world.

Heels of the Ring

Andy Kaufman vs. Jerry Lawler: Andy Kaufman's feud with Jerry Lawler in Memphis Wrestling remains one of the most iconic celebrity angles. Kaufman embraced his role as a heel, taunting the audience and mocking women's wrestling. The rivalry culminated in a legendary match and a fiery segment on *Late Night with David Letterman.*

Beetlejuice vs. Jeff Jarrett: Beetlejuice, the smallest member of Howard Stern's Wack Pack, made a memorable appearance in WCW, where he clashed with Jeff Jarrett. The segment culminated with Jarrett smashing his signature guitar over Beetlejuice's head. The over-the-top moment became a fan-favorite interaction between a celebrity and a wrestling villain.

Wrestling's Villainous History

Professional wrestling has always thrived on the clash between good and evil, and nowhere is this more evident than in the legacy of wrestling's greatest villains. These heels, as they are known in the industry, are more than just adversaries—they are the architects of the drama that keeps fans glued to their screens. For every beloved hero who has inspired cheers, there has been a villain scheming in the shadows, provoking boos and igniting rivalries. From the arrogant taunts of Ric Flair to the unrelenting menace of The Iron Sheik, these villains have perfected the art of being hated, creating storylines that captivate and energize audiences. Their presence doesn't just heighten tension; it defines the emotional stakes of every match, turning athletic contests into battles of good versus evil.

But wrestling villains do more than just antagonize—they elevate the heroes. Hulk Hogan's iconic battles with Andre the Giant and Roddy Piper would not have reached legendary status without the larger-than-life personas of those villains. Stone Cold Steve Austin's rise to superstardom was fueled by his clashes with Vince McMahon, the quintessential corporate heel. Villains challenge the status quo, forcing heroes to overcome not just physical challenges but psychological and moral ones as well. They create stakes, define the boundaries of the conflict, and ultimately make the hero's triumph feel earned. Without them, the world of professional wrestling would lack its emotional intensity, its dramatic edge, and its larger-than-life storytelling.

Beyond their roles in individual storylines, wrestling villains have also mirrored societal fears and anxieties, making them even more impactful. During the Cold War, heels like Nikita Koloff and Ivan Drago capitalized on real-world tensions, transforming geopolitical rivalries into personal grudges. In contrast, the over-the-top arrogance of characters like "Million Dollar Man" Ted DiBiase tapped into class divides, representing wealth and privilege run amok. These villains connected with audiences on a visceral level, embodying the obstacles and antagonists fans faced in their own lives, which made the eventual victories against them all the sweeter.

This section explores the rich history of wrestling's most notorious heels, tracing their impact on the industry and their role in shaping some of wrestling's most unforgettable moments. From the psychological mind games of Jake "The Snake" Roberts to the blatant rule-breaking of Eddie Guerrero, these villains pushed boundaries and challenged conventions. Their ability to provoke emotion—whether through underhanded tactics, scathing promos, or outright cruelty—created moments that transcended the ring. They didn't just make us boo; they made us feel, stirring anger, frustration, and sometimes even reluctant admiration.

In doing so, these villains became an essential part of wrestling's enduring legacy. They ensured that fans stayed invested, week after week, year after year. By embracing their roles as the characters we loved to hate, these heels elevated professional wrestling from mere entertainment to a cultural phenomenon steeped in timeless rivalries and unforgettable drama.

Golden Age of Wrestling Villains

Gorgeous George Ushers in the Era of Charismatic Heels: Gorgeous George revolutionized professional wrestling by transforming it into a spectacle of personality and theatrics. With his elaborate robes, perfectly coiffed hair, and an entourage spraying the ring with "disinfectant," George exuded arrogance. His ability to provoke audiences with both his appearance and biting insults marked a turning point in wrestling, making character work as important as athletic skill. His influence laid the foundation for countless future heels who used personality to draw heat.

Buddy Rogers: The Original Arrogant Champion: "Nature Boy" Buddy Rogers perfected the role of the arrogant heel champion, redefining what it meant to antagonize fans. His cocky strut and signature line, "To a nicer guy, it couldn't happen," fueled audience disdain. Rogers' insistence on flaunting his success and belittling his opponents established him as one of the first wrestlers to embody the idea that a champion could be both despised and compelling. His style became a blueprint for future villains like Ric Flair.

The Sheik and the Birth of Hardcore Villainy: The original Sheik's use of fireballs, pencils, and other foreign objects pushed the boundaries of in-ring violence in the 1960s. His refusal to break character, even outside the ring, added to his mystique and made him a trailblazer in creating fear and loathing. The Sheik's brutal matches inspired the hardcore wrestling style that would emerge decades later, cementing his legacy as a villain who changed the rules of engagement.

Freddie Blassie and the Global Villain Persona: Freddie Blassie's larger-than-life personality and brutal tactics made him a global icon of villainy. Known as "The Hollywood Fashion

Plate," he insulted fans and opponents alike, calling them "pencil-neck geeks." Blassie's bloody matches in Japan earned him the nickname "The Vampire," and his unapologetically violent style captivated and horrified audiences around the world. His ability to adapt his villainy to different cultures showcased the universal appeal of a great heel.

Hans Schmidt and the Post-War Foreign Heel: Portraying a menacing German villain in the aftermath of World War II, Hans Schmidt became one of wrestling's earliest foreign heels. His brutal style and disdain for American audiences made him a lightning rod for fan hatred. Schmidt's persona capitalized on real-world tensions, setting a precedent for villains who mirrored societal fears. His success paved the way for other international heels like The Iron Sheik and Ivan Koloff.

Killer Kowalski and the Infamous Yukon Eric Incident: Killer Kowalski solidified his reputation as one of wrestling's most feared villains when he tore off part of Yukon Eric's ear during a match. The incident became legendary, and Kowalski's sadistic grin afterward only fueled his notoriety. His unapologetic approach to violence made him a trailblazer for heels who embraced their role as ruthless antagonists. This moment defined his career and demonstrated how villains could use real-life injuries to amplify their persona.

The Fabulous Moolah: Dominance Through Deception:
As the longest-reigning women's champion in wrestling history, The Fabulous Moolah relied on underhanded tactics to maintain her dominance. From pulling hair to using the ropes for leverage, Moolah's win-at-all-costs mentality made her a polarizing figure. Her control over women's wrestling extended beyond the ring, as she managed and trained many of her opponents, further cementing her role as a powerful and controversial villain.

Sputnik Monroe: Breaking Rules and Breaking Barriers:
While Sputnik Monroe's legacy is often tied to his efforts to integrate wrestling audiences, his in-ring persona was that of a cocky, rule-breaking heel. Monroe's flashy style and penchant for bending the rules earned him widespread heat, but his real-life actions to fight racial segregation in Memphis wrestling venues made him an icon. His dual legacy as both a villain in

the ring and a hero outside of it remains one of wrestling's most complex stories.

Lou Albano: The Villainous Manager Archetype: Captain Lou Albano redefined the wrestling manager role, turning it into an extension of villainy. Known for his loud, unpredictable promos and constant interference in matches, Albano managed some of the most hated wrestlers of his era. His antics at ringside enraged fans and elevated the wrestlers he represented, making him an integral part of their success and the evolution of managerial roles in wrestling.

Mad Dog Vachon: Unleashing Chaos in the Ring: Mad Dog Vachon's wild and unpredictable style made him one of the most feared heels of his era. Known for biting, clawing, and growling at opponents, Vachon embodied chaos in the ring. His feral persona and violent matches captured the imagination of fans and established him as a standout villain who thrived on unpredictability.

The Evolution of Villains in the 80s & 90s

Ric Flair: The Ultimate Dirtiest Player: Ric Flair embodied the extravagant, arrogant heel of the 1980s with his flashy robes, expensive suits, and braggadocious promos. Declaring himself the "Nature Boy" and proclaiming, "To be the man, you've got to beat the man," Flair cultivated an image of untouchable superiority. His willingness to cheat—whether by using brass knuckles or the ropes for leverage—cemented him as the "Dirtiest Player in the Game," a moniker that resonated across decades.

Ted DiBiase: The Million Dollar Man's Ultimate Power Play: Ted DiBiase brought wealth and corruption into the wrestling ring with his "Million Dollar Man" persona. He famously humiliated fans by offering them cash for degrading tasks, such as kissing his boots or dribbling a basketball, only to cruelly snatch the reward away. DiBiase's purchase of the WWE Championship from Andre the Giant in 1988 shocked fans, redefining how power and villainy could intersect in the wrestling world.

The Iron Sheik and Sgt. Slaughter's Feud: The Iron Sheik's anti-American gimmick evolved in the 1980s as he teamed with Sgt. Slaughter, who turned into an anti-American Iraqi sympathizer during the Gulf War. The betrayal of his patriotic roots made Slaughter one of the most hated heels of the time. Their matches drew immense heat, showcasing how political themes could amplify the role of villains in wrestling.

Jake "The Snake" Roberts: The Master of Psychological Warfare: Jake "The Snake" Roberts didn't rely on brute force alone; he used mind games and cryptic promos to unsettle opponents. His use of Damien, a live python, became an iconic symbol of his villainy, particularly during moments like draping the snake over Randy Savage. Roberts' calculated and cerebral approach to villainy influenced generations of wrestlers.

Mr. Perfect: Arrogance Perfected: Curt Hennig, as Mr. Perfect, lived up to his moniker by presenting himself as flawless in every way. His vignettes showcased his superiority, from bowling strikes to sinking basketball shots effortlessly. In the ring, Hennig's technical prowess and smug attitude made him an infuriating yet captivating villain for fans.

The nWo Revolutionizes Villainy: The New World Order (nWo), led by Hulk Hogan, Scott Hall, and Kevin Nash, shattered wrestling's traditional good-versus-evil dynamics. Hogan's shocking heel turn at *Bash at the Beach 1996* cemented the group as a dominant force. Their rebellious, anti-authority attitude blurred the lines between hero and villain, ushering in a new era of complex, multi-dimensional characters.

Vince McMahon Becomes "Mr. McMahon": Vince McMahon's heel turn during the "Attitude Era" redefined the role of authority figures in wrestling. As the tyrannical boss feuding with Stone Cold Steve Austin, McMahon used his corporate power to stack the deck against Austin at every turn. The feud's popularity skyrocketed WWE's ratings and demonstrated how an antagonist outside the ring could become wrestling's ultimate villain.

The Undertaker's Ministry of Darkness: The Undertaker's evolution into a cult leader with the Ministry of Darkness showcased a darker, more sinister form of villainy. From abducting Stephanie McMahon to attempting "sacrifices" in the ring, the Ministry storyline pushed boundaries. The Undertaker's ominous presence and commitment to the role solidified him as one of wrestling's most unforgettable villains.

The Modern-Day Heel:

Villainy in the PG Era

Roman Reigns: The Tribal Chief Dominates: Roman Reigns reinvented himself as "The Tribal Chief," aligning with Paul Heyman and embracing a villainous persona centered on family dominance and manipulation. His reign as Universal Champion was marked by underhanded tactics, psychological warfare, and brute force. Reigns' transformation from a polarizing face to a universally respected heel demonstrated the modern-day heel's ability to command attention while creating layered, emotionally charged storylines.

Heels of the Ring

MJF: The Pinnacle of Arrogance: Maxwell Jacob Friedman (MJF) has become one of the most effective heels in modern wrestling by weaponizing his sharp wit and unapologetic arrogance. From berating fans to betraying his closest allies, MJF exemplifies villainy that blurs reality and fiction. His ability to provoke genuine animosity from the crowd harks back to the classic heels of old while pushing the boundaries of what a modern antagonist can achieve.

Charlotte Flair: The Queen Reigns Supreme: Charlotte Flair embraced her heritage and natural athleticism to dominate as a heel, using her surname to belittle opponents and elevate her own stature. Her penchant for cheating, including using the ropes for leverage and interference from her father, Ric Flair, solidified her role as a villain. Charlotte's reign as one of the top women's wrestlers exemplifies how modern heels leverage legacy and skill to maintain dominance.

Baron Corbin: The Perfect Mid-Card Villain: Baron Corbin's ability to draw heat stems from his smug attitude and relentless bullying of underdog wrestlers. Whether as "King

Corbin" or the "Lone Wolf," Corbin has leaned into his role as a consistent antagonist, using tactics like interference and post-match beatdowns to cement his heel status. His consistency in provoking audience disdain highlights the importance of mid-card heels in modern wrestling.

Brock Lesnar: The Beast as a Mercenary: Brock Lesnar's limited appearances and reliance on Paul Heyman to deliver scathing promos have enhanced his mystique as a modern-day heel. Lesnar's domination in matches, coupled with brutal attacks on fan favorites like John Cena and Roman Reigns, created an aura of invincibility. His lack of respect for traditional wrestling norms amplified his role as a hated yet compelling villain.

The Miz: The Master of Manipulation: The Miz's career as a heel has been marked by his unmatched ability to manipulate situations to his advantage. Whether exploiting loopholes to retain championships or cutting scathing promos on his rivals, Miz's antics make him one of the most enduring villains of the PG Era. His success in balancing comedy and contempt has kept his character relevant for over a decade.

Alexa Bliss: Twisted Innocence: Alexa Bliss's evolution into a villain aligned with Bray Wyatt's "The Fiend" persona showcased a darker side of her character. Using mind games and eerie psychological tactics, Bliss became a terrifying presence in the women's division. Her unsettling antics, such as hypnotizing opponents and attacking with supernatural elements, set her apart as a unique heel.

Randy Orton: The Apex Predator Strikes Again: Randy Orton's heel turns during the PG Era showcased his ability to bring cold, calculated violence to the forefront. From punting legends like Edge and Christian to betraying his own allies, Orton embodied the persona of a remorseless predator. His longevity and consistency as a top villain cement his status as one of the all-time greats.

The Rise of Anti-Heroes

Stone Cold Steve Austin: The Blueprint for Anti-Heroes: Stone Cold Steve Austin redefined professional wrestling with his rebellious, no-nonsense persona during the Attitude Era. Refusing to follow the rules, Austin's feuds with Vince McMahon highlighted his anti-authority stance, including iconic moments like driving a beer truck into the arena. His ability to blur the lines between hero and villain made him a beloved figure while inspiring a generation of anti-heroes in wrestling.

The Rock: From Villain to Charismatic Anti-Hero: Beginning as a despised heel in the Nation of Domination, The Rock's charisma and sharp wit quickly elevated him to anti-hero status. His biting promos and refusal to pander to fans set him apart as a unique figure who thrived on audience reaction, positive or negative. The Rock's ability to control the crowd with his personality cemented his place as one of wrestling's greatest anti-heroes.

Becky Lynch: The Rise of "The Man": Becky Lynch's journey to anti-hero stardom began with her defiance of WWE's expectations during her feud with Charlotte Flair. Her transformation into "The Man" showcased her unwillingness to conform, delivering fiery promos and standing her ground against authority figures. Fans rallied behind Lynch's unapologetic confidence, making her one of the most significant anti-heroes in modern wrestling.

CM Punk: The Voice of the Voiceless: CM Punk's infamous "Pipe Bomb" promo in 2011 shattered the fourth wall and redefined what it meant to be an anti-hero. By calling out WWE's corporate structure and voicing fans' frustrations,

Punk gained widespread acclaim. His defiance of authority, coupled with his in-ring prowess, solidified his legacy as a revolutionary anti-hero.

Randy Orton: The Tweener Apex Predator: Randy Orton's career has been defined by his ability to shift between hero and villain seamlessly, often occupying the gray area of an anti-hero. His brutal tactics, such as punting opponents or using underhanded strategies, earned him respect and disdain in equal measure. Orton's complex persona embodies the modern anti-hero archetype.

Eddie Guerrero: Lying, Cheating, and Stealing: Eddie Guerrero's "Lie, Cheat, Steal" mantra encapsulated his role as an anti-hero who bent the rules to win. From pretending to be hit by a chair to outsmarting referees, Guerrero's tactics drew laughter and admiration from fans. His charisma and unapologetic approach to bending the rules made him a standout anti-hero in WWE history.

Triple H: The Cerebral Assassin's Dual Roles: Triple H's transition from villainous leader of D-Generation X to a respected anti-hero exemplifies the complexity of his character.

His ruthless strategies and willingness to do whatever it took to win blurred the lines between good and evil. Triple H's evolution showcased the duality of an anti-hero, capable of commanding both boos and cheers.

Roman Reigns: The Evolution to Tribal Chief: Roman Reigns' transformation from polarizing face to dominant anti-hero with his "Tribal Chief" persona highlights the modern evolution of wrestling characters. While undeniably a villain, Reigns' aura, family loyalty, and manipulation of opponents have garnered reluctant admiration. His ability to command respect and loathing in equal measure embodies the essence of an anti-hero.

How Villains Reflect Society's Fears

The Iron Sheik: Cold War Hostility: The Iron Sheik's anti-American persona during the Cold War capitalized on real-world fears of foreign threats. Waving the Iranian flag and using his signature Camel Clutch submission hold, he symbolized geopolitical tensions. His villainy served as a catharsis for fans, allowing them to rally behind American heroes like Hulk Hogan.

Muhammad Hassan: Post-9/11 Anxiety: Muhammad Hassan's character debuted as a critic of American xenophobia but quickly morphed into a controversial heel representing anti-American sentiment. His promos highlighted societal fears and prejudices, leading to intense reactions from audiences. The character's abrupt retirement underscored the difficulty of navigating sensitive topics in wrestling.

The Anti-American Alliance of the 1980s: Tag teams like The Bolsheviks and wrestlers such as Nikolai Volkoff used Cold War fears to incite audience anger. Their performances, including Volkoff's singing of the Soviet national anthem, reflected the political climate of the time. These villains turned real-world tensions into dramatic in-ring confrontations.

Bray Wyatt's Cult-Like Manipulation: Drawing on fears of charismatic leaders and societal vulnerabilities, Bray Wyatt's character exploited themes of psychological control. His eerie demeanor and cryptic promos mirrored real-world anxieties about cults and manipulation. Wyatt's persona resonated as a symbol of unseen dangers lurking in society.

The Undertaker's Supernatural Threats: The Undertaker's early character leaned heavily on fears of death and the afterlife. With his dark attire, eerie music, and somber demeanor, he represented humanity's primal fear of mortality. His storylines often revolved around supernatural elements, giving audiences a safe way to confront their anxieties.

The Mountie: Authority Figures as Villains: The Mountie's gimmick as a corrupt Canadian law enforcement officer reflected societal fears of abuse of power. From using his cattle prod to humiliating opponents, he embodied the anxieties surrounding unchecked authority. His antics drew boos while tapping into a universal distrust of corrupt officials.

The Fiend: Wrestling's Manifestation of Trauma: Bray Wyatt's "Fiend" persona represented fears of inner demons and unresolved trauma. His grotesque mask and violent tactics embodied psychological horror, resonating with fans on a deeper, subconscious level. The Fiend's storylines often explored themes of redemption and revenge, mirroring societal struggles with mental health.

Doink the Clown: Subverting Innocence: Originally portrayed as a sinister heel, Doink the Clown played on coulrophobia, or fear of clowns. His pranks often turned cruel, unsettling audiences who expected clowns to be harmless. This darker portrayal reflected the unease people feel when familiar symbols of joy take a sinister turn.

Papa Shango: Supernatural Anxiety: Papa Shango's voodoo practitioner gimmick tapped into fears of the unknown and the occult. His eerie rituals and "curses" on opponents added a layer of supernatural tension to his matches. The character's over-the-top presentation reflected societal fascination and fear of the mystical.

La Resistance: Post-9/11 Global Tensions: The French-Canadian tag team La Resistance debuted as heels criticizing American foreign policy. Their anti-American rhetoric and smug attitudes provoked strong reactions, reflecting the global tensions of the early 2000s. Their matches often felt like a microcosm of larger geopolitical debates.

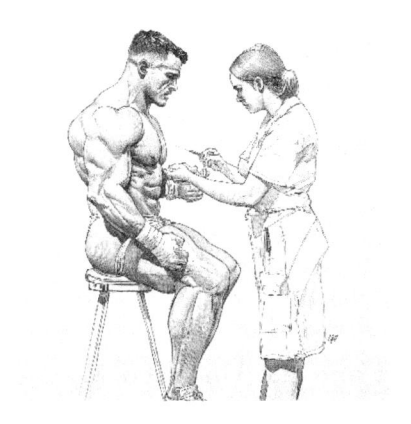

Villains Outside the Ring:

Public Scandals and Controversies

Hulk Hogan's Racist Remarks: In 2015, Hulk Hogan was embroiled in controversy after recordings of his racist comments surfaced. WWE severed ties with Hogan, removing him from the Hall of Fame and erasing his legacy from their programming. Though later reinstated, the scandal tarnished Hogan's reputation and divided fans.

The Chris Benoit Tragedy: In 2007, Chris Benoit's double murder-suicide shocked the wrestling world and prompted scrutiny of the industry's physical and mental toll. The tragedy led to widespread discussions about concussions, drug use, and mental health, casting a dark shadow over Benoit's once-celebrated career.

Jimmy Snuka and the Unsolved Mystery: WWE Hall of Famer Jimmy Snuka faced renewed scrutiny in 2015 for the 1983 death of his girlfriend, Nancy Argentino. Though initially ruled accidental, the case was reopened, and Snuka was charged with third-degree murder. The trial was later dismissed due to Snuka's declining health, but the controversy marred his legacy.

The Steroid Scandal of the 1990s: Vince McMahon and WWE faced legal battles in the early 1990s over the alleged distribution of steroids to wrestlers. The trial, which included testimony from Hulk Hogan, exposed the widespread use of performance-enhancing drugs in the industry. While McMahon was acquitted, the scandal damaged WWE's public image.

Ric Flair's "Plane Ride from Hell": During the infamous "Plane Ride from Hell" in 2002, Ric Flair was accused of exposing himself and harassing a flight attendant. The allegations, revealed in a 2021 documentary, reignited scrutiny of Flair's behavior and led to significant backlash. While Flair has denied the accusations, his once-untouchable reputation has suffered lasting damage.

Jeff Hardy's Legal Troubles: Jeff Hardy's battles with addiction and multiple arrests have been well-documented. From DUIs to drug possession charges, Hardy's struggles have impacted his career and personal life. Despite numerous comebacks, his legal issues remain a recurring challenge.

Alberto Del Rio's Legal Battles: Alberto Del Rio was arrested in 2020 on charges of assault and kidnapping after an alleged altercation with a partner. Though the charges were later dropped due to insufficient evidence, the allegations severely tarnished Del Rio's reputation. Once a top star in WWE, his career has yet to recover from the fallout.

Sunny's Fall from Grace: WWE Hall of Famer Sunny, real name Tammy Sytch, has faced repeated legal troubles, including DUIs, parole violations, and fraud charges. In 2022, she was involved in a car accident that resulted in a fatality, leading to charges of DUI manslaughter. Once celebrated as a trailblazer for women in wrestling, her legal issues now overshadow her legacy.

Enzo Amore's Assault Allegations: Enzo Amore was released from WWE in 2018 following allegations of assault, though the case was later dropped due to insufficient evidence. The controversy ended his WWE career and highlighted the challenges of navigating personal scandals in the public eye.

Jake "The Snake" Roberts' Struggles with Addiction: Jake Roberts' battles with substance abuse were well-documented, including moments captured in the documentary *The Resurrection of Jake the Snake*. His eventual recovery inspired fans, but his struggles remain a cautionary tale about the toll of the wrestling lifestyle.

Marty Jannetty's Confessional Controversy: In 2020, Marty Jannetty posted a cryptic social media message suggesting he had committed a murder in his youth. Although he later claimed it was part of a storyline, the post sparked a police investigation. The bizarre incident added to Jannetty's reputation for erratic behavior.

Scott Hall's Public Struggles: Known as Razor Ramon, Scott Hall's battles with addiction and public incidents, including arrests and rehab stints, were well-documented. Despite his personal struggles, Hall's journey of recovery inspired fans, though his reputation was often overshadowed by controversy.

Velveteen Dream's Allegations of Misconduct: Velveteen Dream, real name Patrick Clark, was accused of inappropriate behavior involving minors in 2020. Though he denied the allegations, the controversy led to his release from WWE and significant damage to his once-promising career. Dream's fall from grace serves as a cautionary tale about the importance of personal conduct.

Bill DeMott's Allegations of Abuse: Former WWE trainer Bill DeMott faced multiple allegations of misconduct during his tenure at the Performance Center, including claims of physical intimidation, verbal abuse, and fostering a toxic training environment. Several trainees reported inappropriate drills, such as forcing wrestlers to perform dangerous moves or endure excessive physical punishment as "discipline." The public outcry from former trainees ultimately led to his resignation in 2015, sparking conversations about the need for safer and more professional training practices in wrestling.

Infamous Feuds:

When Villains Took It Too Far?

Randy Orton vs. Triple H: Breaking into the McMahon Home: During their intense feud in 2009, Randy Orton crossed a line when he "broke into" Triple H and Stephanie McMahon's home as part of a storyline. The invasion blurred the line between fiction and reality, with Orton smashing objects and threatening violence. The segment's shocking nature heightened the stakes of their WrestleMania 25 match but also drew criticism for its extreme portrayal.

The Undertaker vs. Mankind: Hell in a Cell 1998: The Undertaker and Mankind's legendary feud culminated in their Hell in a Cell match, where Mankind was thrown off the top of the cell. The fall, coupled with Mankind's later plunge through the cell roof, shocked fans and demonstrated the physical extremes of their rivalry. The match became an iconic yet brutal representation of pushing boundaries in wrestling.

Edge vs. Matt Hardy: Blurring Real-Life Betrayal: When Matt Hardy's real-life breakup with Lita became public, WWE turned it into a storyline involving Edge. The feud brought raw emotion and legitimate animosity into the ring, with Hardy accusing Edge of betraying their friendship. The angle's personal nature captivated fans but also risked pushing boundaries of professional ethics.

Triple H vs. Kane: The Katie Vick Controversy: In one of WWE's most infamous storylines, Triple H accused Kane of being involved in the fictional death of Katie Vick. The angle included tasteless skits and sparked backlash from fans and critics alike. This feud highlighted how pushing shock value can sometimes alienate audiences.

CM Punk vs. Jeff Hardy: Addiction as a Weapon: CM Punk's rivalry with Jeff Hardy in 2009 saw Punk targeting Hardy's real-life struggles with addiction. Punk's promos, including accusations of irresponsibility and self-destruction, struck a nerve with fans. While the feud elevated Punk as a villain, its reliance on personal issues made it uncomfortably intense.

Ric Flair vs. Dusty Rhodes: Breaking the American Dream: Ric Flair and Dusty Rhodes' rivalry was steeped in class warfare, with Flair mocking Rhodes' working-class roots. The feud intensified when Flair and the Four Horsemen broke Rhodes' ankle, symbolically "breaking the American Dream." The storyline captured fans' imaginations, cementing Flair as a detestable villain.

Jake "The Snake" Roberts vs. Randy Savage: The Cobra Bite: Jake Roberts took his villainy to new heights by unleashing a live cobra on Randy Savage during a televised segment. The snake bit Savage's arm, leaving fans horrified and cementing Roberts' reputation as a master of psychological warfare. The shocking moment remains one of the most talked-about acts of villainy in wrestling history.

The Rock vs. Mankind: Chair Shots Heard Around the World: In their *I Quit* match at the 1999 Royal Rumble, The Rock delivered an unrelenting series of chair shots to Mankind while he was handcuffed. The brutal assault shocked fans and left Mankind visibly injured, highlighting the lengths villains could go to assert dominance. The match remains controversial for its excessive violence.

Hulk Hogan vs. Randy Savage: The Mega Powers Explode: Hulk Hogan and Randy Savage's friendship disintegrated in a feud that centered on jealousy and betrayal. Savage accused Hogan of coveting Miss Elizabeth, leading to their epic clash at WrestleMania V. The storyline's emotional stakes made it one of the most memorable rivalries of the 1980s.

Eddie Guerrero vs. Rey Mysterio: The Custody of Dominik: Eddie Guerrero's heel turn during his feud with Rey Mysterio reached its climax in a ladder match for custody of

Rey's son Dominik. Guerrero's manipulative tactics and emotional promos added drama to the feud, making it one of the most unique storylines in wrestling history.

Villains Who Became Heroes

The Rock: From Arrogance to Electrifying: Initially debuting as the smug and arrogant "Rocky Maivia," The Rock was reviled by fans for his overconfidence. However, after embracing his heel persona in The Nation of Domination, his sharp wit and unmatched charisma turned boos into cheers. By the time he left The Nation, The Rock had transformed into "The People's Champion," one of the most beloved wrestlers in history.

Triple H: From Cerebral Assassin to Respected Leader: Known for his villainous tactics as the leader of DX and Evolution, Triple H spent years as WWE's top heel. However, his transition to an elder statesman and authority figure on NXT earned him respect and admiration from fans. Triple H's dedication to developing young talent has solidified his status as a hero in the wrestling world.

Randy Orton: The Legend Killer Turns Mentor: As the "Legend Killer," Randy Orton took pride in disrespecting and defeating WWE's most revered figures. Over time, however, his longevity and dedication to the business earned him a new level of respect. His role mentoring younger stars like Riddle showcased a more relatable and heroic side to the once ruthless villain.

Eddie Guerrero: Lie, Cheat, Steal, and Love: Eddie Guerrero's heel tactics of lying, cheating, and stealing made him a despised villain early in his WWE career. Yet, fans began to cheer for his clever antics and undeniable charm. Guerrero's journey culminated in his WWE Championship win, solidifying him as a fan-favorite hero whose legacy remains cherished.

Heels of the Ring

Becky Lynch: The Man Breaks Through: Becky Lynch's journey from overlooked competitor to "The Man" began with a heel turn against Charlotte Flair. Her newfound confidence and no-nonsense attitude resonated with fans, who embraced her as a symbol of empowerment. Lynch's rise from villain to hero redefined women's wrestling.

Kane: The Monster Becomes Mayor: Introduced as The Undertaker's menacing and destructive brother, Kane terrorized WWE for years. However, his willingness to embrace comedic roles and his dedication to public service as Mayor Glenn Jacobs showcased a softer, more heroic side. Kane's transformation from monster to admired figure is one of wrestling's most unexpected.

The Miz: From Reality Star Heel to Respected Veteran: Initially despised for his brash personality and reality TV background, The Miz became one of WWE's most consistent heels. Over time, his dedication and work ethic earned him the respect of fans and peers alike. His heartfelt promo after winning the WWE Championship in 2021 exemplified his transformation into a respected figure.

Batista: From Evolution Enforcer to Hollywood Hero: Batista's early career as Evolution's enforcer showcased his brutal, villainous side. However, his eventual split from the faction and pursuit of the WWE Championship highlighted his heroic qualities. Batista's transition to Hollywood further endeared him to fans, solidifying his status as a beloved figure.

CM Punk: Anti-Hero to Voice of the People: CM Punk's initial heel runs were defined by his cutting promos and abrasive personality. However, his "Voice of the Voiceless" era saw fans rallying behind his fight against WWE's corporate structure. Punk's ability to channel real frustrations into his character blurred the lines between hero and villain.

Roman Reigns: From Booed Hero to Tribal Chief: Roman Reigns' villainous Tribal Chief persona revitalized his career and made him one of WWE's most compelling characters. Fans have gradually begun to admire his dominance and charisma, showcasing how a well-executed villain run can lead to heroic redemption.

Villain Archetypes

In the world of professional wrestling, not all villains are created equal. Wrestling's most compelling heels are built on archetypes—timeless character molds that resonate with audiences by tapping into universal fears, frustrations, and even grudging admiration. These archetypes define the personas of villains, giving them the depth and identity needed to stand out and leave a lasting impact. Whether they are smug intellectuals lording their superiority over the crowd, unrelenting monsters fueled by destruction, or sneaky opportunists willing to stoop to any low, these villains embody traits that evoke strong emotional responses from fans. They are the cornerstones of storytelling, each with a distinct role to play in the drama of the squared circle.

Wrestling's villain archetypes have evolved over time, adapting to cultural shifts and audience expectations. The arrogant aristocrats of the 1980s, like the "Million Dollar Man" Ted DiBiase, reflected class struggles and societal frustrations with the ultra-wealthy. Meanwhile, silent giants like Andre the Giant or The Great Khali leaned into primal fears of overwhelming physical dominance. Modern wrestling continues to refine these archetypes, introducing complex anti-heroes like Seth Rollins or Bray Wyatt, who blur the lines between villainy and misunderstood genius. These archetypes transcend generations, remaining as relevant today as they were in the golden age of wrestling.

What makes these archetypes so enduring is their versatility. A conniving villain can cheat to win one night and cut a scathing promo the next, always finding new ways to provoke anger or disdain. The monster heel can intimidate and destroy in one feud but reveal surprising vulnerability in another, adding layers to their persona. The best villains aren't static; they adapt, evolve, and continually find new ways to torment heroes and enrage fans. By drawing from these archetypes, wrestling creates characters that feel larger than life while remaining grounded in universal human traits.

In this section, we'll delve into the archetypes that have defined wrestling's most memorable villains. From the unstoppable giants who dominated with brute strength to the cocky showboats who taunted their way into infamy, these archetypes offer a fascinating glimpse into the psychology of wrestling storytelling. We'll explore the tropes, traits, and tactics that make each archetype unique, as well as the legendary figures who brought them to life.

Through their actions, words, and sheer presence, these archetypal villains didn't just antagonize—they captivated. By embodying familiar fears and frustrations, they forged connections with audiences that transcended the ring. Each archetype played a role in shaping wrestling's legacy, ensuring that the drama stayed compelling, and the heroes had something truly formidable to overcome. As we step into the realm of wrestling's villain archetypes, prepare to meet the characters who made us cheer for their defeat and, occasionally, admire their craft.

The Arrogant Villain:

Flaunting Wealth and Power

Few archetypes in professional wrestling elicit as much disdain as the arrogant villain. These heels thrive on flaunting their wealth, power, and superiority, belittling fans and opponents alike. Their finely tailored suits, lavish entrances, and endless taunts serve one purpose: to remind everyone else of their supposed inferiority. By rubbing their excess and privilege in audiences' faces, these villains tap into universal frustrations about inequality and entitlement, making them some of the most despised characters in wrestling history.

"Million Dollar Man" Ted DiBiase

Ted DiBiase epitomized the archetype of the arrogant villain during the late 1980s and early 1990s. His character revolved around the idea that everyone had a price, and he used his wealth to humiliate others both inside and outside the ring. Whether it was paying a child to dribble a basketball—only to kick it away at the last moment—or buying his way into championship opportunities, DiBiase's antics made fans loathe him. The crowning symbol of his arrogance was the Million Dollar Championship, a title he created solely to showcase his wealth and power. DiBiase's ability to make audiences detest him cemented his legacy as one of wrestling's greatest villains.

Ric Flair

The "Nature Boy" Ric Flair brought arrogance to a new level with his trademark robes, expensive watches, and endless boasts about his "jet-flying, limousine-riding" lifestyle. Flair's over-the-top persona was matched by his in-ring brilliance, allowing him to back up his claims of superiority. His catchphrase, "To be the man, you've got to beat the man," became a rallying cry for his dominance. Flair's feuds often centered on his flaunting wealth and belittling his opponents, making him a quintessential arrogant villain who earned as many boos as he did begrudging respect.

JBL (John Bradshaw Layfield)

JBL's transformation from beer-drinking brawler to wealthy Texan tycoon in the mid-2000s exemplified the arrogant villain archetype. He relished in insulting fans for their supposed lack of sophistication and often exploited his financial resources to gain an edge in matches. JBL's WWE Championship reign was marked by underhanded tactics and condescending promos, such as riding into arenas in a limousine and cutting elaborate speeches about his superiority. His character became a lightning rod for fan hatred, solidifying his place as a master of this archetype.

Alberto Del Rio

Alberto Del Rio debuted in WWE as a smug aristocrat who believed he was destined for greatness. Arriving in luxurious cars and flanked by his personal ring announcer, Del Rio exuded an air of entitlement that grated on audiences. His condescending smile and tendency to berate his opponents made him a natural heel. Del Rio's persona was steeped in the arrogance of inherited wealth and privilege, making every one of his defeats feel satisfying to fans.

MJF (Maxwell Jacob Friedman)

One of the modern era's most effective arrogant villains, MJF embodies entitlement and superiority in every aspect of his character. From belittling fans with razor-sharp insults to flaunting his designer scarves and custom suits, MJF spares no opportunity to remind audiences of his self-proclaimed greatness. His heel work is so convincing that even in an era where fans often cheer villains, MJF consistently draws pure hatred. His ability to manipulate emotions and maintain his arrogant persona makes him a standout example of this archetype.

Concluding Thoughts

The arrogant villain archetype endures because it taps into real-world frustrations with wealth, privilege, and entitlement. These characters force fans to confront their own grievances while providing larger-than-life personalities to direct their boos toward. These villains have made arrogance an art form, ensuring their place as some of wrestling's most memorable antagonists.

The Sadistic Villain:

Thriving on Pain and Suffering

Some villains thrive not just on winning but on inflicting as much pain as possible along the way. These sadistic heels are defined by their brutality, often savoring the suffering of their opponents. They use violence as a tool to dominate and terrify, leaving audiences in awe and disgust. These characters blur the line between competitor and tormentor, making them some of the most chilling figures in wrestling history.

Jake "The Snake" Roberts

Jake Roberts was a master of psychological torment, using both his words and actions to strike fear into his opponents. Known for carrying his signature snake, Damien, to the ring, Roberts' most sadistic moments included unleashing the reptile on unsuspecting victims. His calm, calculating promos only amplified his menacing aura, making fans and wrestlers alike uneasy. The infamous moment when he had a cobra bite Randy Savage epitomized Roberts' willingness to push boundaries, solidifying his place as a sadistic villain.

New Jack

In the world of extreme wrestling, few figures are as controversial as New Jack. Known for his unrelenting violence in ECW, New Jack blurred the line between performance and reality. Armed with weapons like staple guns, baseball bats wrapped in barbed wire, and even a shopping cart full of tools, he inflicted gruesome injuries on his opponents. His infamous "Mass Transit" incident showcased his penchant for going too far, leaving fans divided over whether he was a performer or a danger.

Heels of the Ring

The Fiend (Bray Wyatt)

The Fiend brought a terrifying, sadistic presence to WWE that left fans both horrified and mesmerized. Donning a nightmarish mask and attacking opponents with unrelenting brutality, The Fiend thrived on psychological warfare. His attacks on Finn Bálor, Seth Rollins, and Daniel Bryan often left them physically and emotionally shattered. The Fiend's eerie character blurred the line between monster and man, making him one of WWE's most unsettling villains.

Abdullah the Butcher

Abdullah the Butcher became infamous for his hardcore style and love of bloodshed. Using weapons like forks and spikes, he left his opponents battered and bloodied in matches that often resembled brawls more than wrestling contests. Abdullah's unpredictability and willingness to take violence to the extreme made him a legend in territories across the globe, earning him the nickname "The Madman from the Sudan."

Randy Orton

Known as "The Legend Killer," Randy Orton's sadistic streak defined many of his early feuds. His willingness to punt opponents in the head, leaving them "injured," showcased his ruthlessness. Orton's calculated attacks on legends like Mick Foley and Ric Flair demonstrated his thirst for dominance, solidifying him as one of WWE's most dangerous heels. His sadistic tendencies have continued to resurface throughout his career, making him a constant threat.

Concluding Thoughts

Sadistic villains thrive on pushing boundaries and inflicting suffering, making them unforgettable forces of chaos in wrestling. Whether through psychological manipulation or physical brutality, these heels leave an indelible mark on their opponents and fans. The sadistic villain archetype ensures that wrestling remains as visceral and unpredictable as ever.

The Cowardly Villain:

Avoiding Conflict at All Costs

The cowardly villain is one of wrestling's most enduring archetypes, designed to infuriate fans by refusing to fight fairly. These heels specialize in sneak attacks, interference, and outright avoidance of conflict when the odds aren't in their favor. Their actions, while despicable, serve to amplify the hero's journey, as fans eagerly anticipate the moment the coward finally gets what's coming to them. Despite their underhanded tactics, cowardly villains are master storytellers, using their antics to build tension and elevate the stakes of every match.

Heels of the Ring

Bobby "The Brain" Heenan

Bobby Heenan wasn't just a manager; he was also one of wrestling's greatest cowardly heels. Known for his quick wit and even quicker exits, Heenan excelled at provoking heroes and fans alike, only to flee when confronted. His antics during matches—from distracting referees to interfering on behalf of his clients—were legendary. Heenan's cowardice added layers of humor and frustration to his character, cementing his legacy as the quintessential sneaky villain.

The Miz

Few wrestlers have embodied cowardice as effectively as The Miz. Throughout his career, The Miz has been known for ducking challenges, relying on interference from allies, and taking cheap shots whenever possible. A standout example came during his WWE Championship reign in 2010-2011, when he repeatedly escaped matches with disqualifications and count-outs. The Miz's ability to frustrate opponents and fans alike has made him one of the most enduring cowardly villains in modern wrestling.

Honky Tonk Man

The Honky Tonk Man's record-setting Intercontinental Championship reign wasn't built on dominance but on cowardly tactics. He often relied on count-outs, disqualifications, and outside interference to retain his title. His exaggerated Elvis impersonation and grating personality only added to the fans' desire to see him finally lose. When The Ultimate Warrior squashed him in seconds at *SummerSlam 1988*, it marked one of the most satisfying comeuppances for a cowardly heel.

Seth Rollins

During his run as WWE Champion in 2015, Seth Rollins epitomized the cowardly villain archetype. Despite his undeniable in-ring talent, Rollins consistently relied on interference from The Authority and sneaky tactics to retain his title. His willingness to flee from fights and manipulate situations to his advantage made fans despise him even more. Rollins' cowardly antics elevated his eventual defeats, making them all the more rewarding.

"Hollywood" Hulk Hogan

When Hulk Hogan turned heel and joined the nWo, he reinvented himself as a conniving and cowardly villain. Despite his legendary status, Hogan frequently avoided direct confrontations, relying on his nWo allies to do his dirty work. His infamous habit of bailing out of matches when the odds turned against him frustrated fans and cemented his place as one of wrestling's most notorious cowardly heels.

Concluding Thoughts

The cowardly villain archetype thrives on frustration, delivering moments of tension and anticipation that make the hero's victory even sweeter. These heels have mastered the art of avoidance, proving that sometimes, running away is just as compelling as standing tall in the ring.

The Foreign Threat:

Playing on National Fears

The "foreign menace" archetype is one of the most controversial yet enduring tropes in wrestling history. These villains, often portrayed as representing a nation perceived as an adversary, play on societal fears and geopolitical tensions. Through their accents, attire, and antagonistic personas, they provoke strong reactions from audiences, uniting fans in their support of the homegrown hero. While this archetype reflects the time periods in which these characters thrived, it also underscores wrestling's ability to evoke intense emotions by mirroring real-world anxieties.

The Iron Sheik

The Iron Sheik became one of the most iconic foreign villains in wrestling during the 1980s, capitalizing on real-world tensions between the United States and Iran. His anti-American promos, coupled with his use of the Camel Clutch submission hold, made him an instant heel. The Sheik's rivalry with Hulk Hogan, culminating in Hogan's victory for the WWE Championship, is often credited with launching the golden era of professional wrestling. The Sheik's ability to enrage crowds while maintaining his character's authenticity made him a master of the foreign menace archetype.

Nikita Koloff

Dubbed "The Russian Nightmare," Nikita Koloff represented Soviet dominance during the Cold War era. With his imposing physique and no-nonsense demeanor, Koloff embodied the fear of a seemingly unstoppable foreign adversary. His feud with Dusty Rhodes played on the ideological battle between communism and the American Dream, creating matches that were as much about storytelling as they were about athleticism. Koloff's eventual face turn showed the archetype's versatility, as he transitioned from villain to beloved hero.

Jinder Mahal

Jinder Mahal's rise as WWE Champion in 2017 was steeped in his portrayal as an anti-American foreign menace. Mahal frequently insulted the fans' values while aligning himself with his homeland's traditions, declaring himself superior to American culture. His reliance on his associates, The Singh Brothers, further emphasized his villainous tactics. Mahal's reign, while divisive among fans, demonstrated how the foreign menace archetype could be modernized for a globalized wrestling audience.

Tiger Jeet Singh

Tiger Jeet Singh's career as a foreign menace spanned territories in both North America and Japan. His wild, unpredictable persona and use of weapons like swords created an aura of danger and chaos. Singh's feuds with wrestling legends like Antonio Inoki in Japan and Bruno Sammartino in the U.S. showcased his ability to evoke fear and hatred from audiences. His success in multiple markets highlights the archetype's universal appeal.

Yokozuna

Although billed as a sumo wrestler from Japan, Yokozuna was actually of Samoan descent, but his portrayal leaned heavily into traditional Japanese stereotypes. Managed by Mr. Fuji, Yokozuna dominated WWE with his sheer size and power, becoming a two-time WWE Champion. His matches against American icons like Hulk Hogan and Lex Luger were framed as battles of cultural pride, with Yokozuna's villainy symbolizing an external threat to American values. Despite the controversy surrounding his character's portrayal, Yokozuna remains one of the most memorable heels in wrestling history.

Concluding Thoughts

The foreign menace archetype has often reflected the fears and tensions of its era, making these villains both timely and impactful. While the trope has evolved to be more nuanced in modern wrestling, its ability to generate emotion and rally fans behind a hero remains unparalleled. These villains have left an indelible mark on the industry by embodying the external threats that fuel wrestling's timeless battle between good and evil.

The Monster Heel:

Destroying Everything in Their Path

Few archetypes in professional wrestling are as awe-inspiring and terrifying as the monster heel. These towering, unstoppable forces of destruction thrive on their sheer physical dominance, using their size and strength to crush opponents and intimidate fans. Monster heels are a staple of wrestling, providing larger-than-life obstacles for heroes to overcome. Their appeal lies in their primal power and ability to instill fear, creating high-stakes drama that captivates audiences.

Andre the Giant

Andre the Giant's immense size and strength made him a natural fit for the monster heel archetype. While he began his career as a beloved attraction, his heel turn against Hulk Hogan in the mid-1980s transformed him into one of wrestling's most feared villains. Aligning with Bobby Heenan, Andre's betrayal set up the legendary WrestleMania III match, where Hogan's victory symbolized the ultimate triumph over an insurmountable foe. Andre's aura of invincibility and his ability to dominate the ring cemented his place as the definitive monster heel.

Big Van Vader

Known for his agility despite his massive size, Big Van Vader brought an unparalleled intensity to the monster heel role. Competing in WCW, WWE, and Japan, Vader terrorized his opponents with brutal moves like the Vader Bomb and a devastating powerbomb. His rivalries with Sting and Ric Flair showcased his ability to elevate the stakes of any match. Vader's combination of raw power and athleticism made him one of the most feared competitors of his era.

Yokozuna

Yokozuna embodied the monster heel archetype with his imposing size and unrelenting dominance. Managed by Mr. Fuji, Yokozuna's matches often ended with the devastating Banzai Drop, leaving his opponents crushed and defeated. His victories over legends like Hulk Hogan and Bret Hart solidified his status as an unstoppable force in WWE during the early 1990s. Yokozuna's reign of terror was a defining period for the monster heel archetype.

The Undertaker

While The Undertaker evolved into a fan-favorite over his career, his early years in WWE showcased him as a terrifying monster heel. Accompanied by Paul Bearer and wielding an otherworldly presence, The Undertaker dominated his opponents with chilling precision. His feuds with Hulk Hogan and Ultimate Warrior emphasized his invincibility, while his signature Tombstone Piledriver became one of the most feared moves in wrestling. The Undertaker's mystique and destructive power set a new standard for monster heels.

Braun Strowman

A modern example of the monster heel, Braun Strowman's raw strength and ability to perform incredible feats of power have made him a standout. From flipping ambulances to destroying entire sets, Strowman's displays of dominance captivated fans. His rivalries with Roman Reigns and Brock Lesnar highlighted his ability to stand toe-to-toe with the best. Strowman's combination of physicality and presence ensures the monster heel archetype remains relevant in contemporary wrestling.

Concluding Thoughts

The monster heel archetype embodies the timeless appeal of larger-than-life villains, providing a physical and psychological challenge for wrestling heroes. These towering figures have defined some of wrestling's most iconic moments. Their ability to dominate the ring and instill fear ensures their place as enduring symbols of power and menace in professional wrestling.

The Charismatic Villain:

Winning with Words

Charisma can be a powerful weapon, and in professional wrestling, the charismatic villain uses words as effectively as others use brute strength. These heels captivate audiences with their wit, eloquence, and ability to manipulate emotions. Whether through scathing promos, biting insults, or even humor, charismatic villains blur the line between love and hate. Fans may despise their actions, but they cannot help but hang on every word, making these villains unforgettable figures in the world of wrestling.

Ric Flair

Few wrestlers have wielded charisma as effectively as Ric Flair. The "Nature Boy" combined his larger-than-life persona with eloquent, often brash, promos that cemented his place as one of wrestling's greatest talkers. Flair's catchphrases, like "To be the man, you've got to beat the man," became iconic. His ability to gloat about his wealth, accomplishments, and lifestyle while simultaneously belittling his opponents made him the archetype for the charismatic villain. Flair's unmatched ability to provoke both admiration and hatred ensured that he stayed relevant for decades.

Chris Jericho

Chris Jericho's career has been defined by his unparalleled ability to reinvent himself while remaining one of wrestling's most entertaining villains. From creating "The List of Jericho" to calling himself the "Ayatollah of Rock 'n' Rolla," Jericho has a gift for blending humor with cutting insults. His promo skills have helped elevate feuds with legends like The Rock and Shawn Michaels, and his ability to connect with fans while playing the villain is unmatched. Jericho's charisma has made him a beloved figure despite his villainous antics.

Heels of the Ring

MJF (Maxwell Jacob Friedman)

In the modern era, few villains have mastered the art of charisma like MJF. Known for his scathing insults and unrelenting arrogance, MJF excels at antagonizing both his opponents and the audience. His promos are sharp, unfiltered, and unapologetically villainous, often blurring the line between kayfabe and reality. MJF's ability to maintain his heel persona both on and off-screen has solidified his place as one of the most captivating talkers in wrestling today.

"Rowdy" Roddy Piper

Roddy Piper's quick wit and fiery promos made him one of wrestling's most compelling villains. As the host of "Piper's Pit," he created memorable moments by verbally dismantling his guests before escalating to physical confrontations. Piper's feud with Hulk Hogan leading up to the first WrestleMania showcased his ability to sell a storyline with nothing more than his words. His charisma and unpredictability kept fans hooked, even as they hated him.

Paul Heyman

Though not an in-ring competitor, Paul Heyman's promo skills have elevated countless wrestlers, from Brock Lesnar to Roman Reigns. As a manager and advocate, Heyman's silver tongue has made him one of wrestling's most effective villains. His ability to blend eloquence with manipulation ensures that every word he speaks carries weight. Whether boasting about Lesnar's dominance or proclaiming Reigns as the "Tribal Chief," Heyman's promos have defined many of wrestling's most compelling storylines.

Concluding Thoughts

Charismatic villains prove that words can be just as powerful as physical strength in wrestling. These heels captivate audiences with their wit, confidence, and ability to manipulate emotions, creating moments that resonate far beyond the ring. Charismatic villains ensure that wrestling remains as much about storytelling as it is about competition.

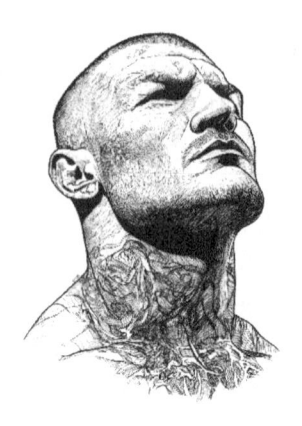

Villains Who Blurred the Lines:

Anti-Hero Heels

Not all villains are created equal. Some defy traditional definitions of good and evil, operating in a morally gray area that makes them as intriguing as they are unpredictable. These anti-hero heels often display traits of both villains and heroes, earning boos and cheers in equal measure. Their unpredictability, complex motivations, and willingness to challenge the status quo make them some of the most compelling characters in wrestling history. Fans may hate their methods, but they often admire their resolve, leaving a lasting impact on the sport.

Stone Cold Steve Austin

Stone Cold Steve Austin's rise to prominence during the Attitude Era blurred the lines between hero and villain. His defiance of authority, particularly his iconic clashes with Vince McMahon, resonated with fans who saw him as a working-class hero. However, Austin's methods—from attacking opponents with steel chairs to breaking every rule in the book—were undeniably villainous. His anti-hero persona redefined what it meant to be a wrestling protagonist, making him one of the most popular and complex characters in WWE history.

Eddie Guerrero

Eddie Guerrero's "Lie, Cheat, and Steal" persona perfectly encapsulated the anti-hero archetype. While his tactics were underhanded, Guerrero's charisma and humor endeared him to fans. His clever ways of outsmarting opponents, such as pretending to be hit by a steel chair to get a disqualification win, showcased his ability to bend the rules in his favor. Eddie's mix of villainous behavior and undeniable charm made him a beloved yet mischievous figure in wrestling.

Becky Lynch

Becky Lynch's transformation into "The Man" saw her embrace an anti-hero edge that propelled her to superstardom.

Her initial heel turn against Charlotte Flair backfired, as fans embraced her no-nonsense attitude and refusal to conform to traditional hero tropes. Lynch's willingness to stand up for herself and take bold actions—even at the expense of friendships—made her a trailblazer who blurred the lines between hero and villain.

CM Punk

CM Punk's "Pipe Bomb" promo in 2011 marked a turning point in his career, positioning him as an anti-hero who spoke uncomfortable truths about WWE's corporate culture. While his words and actions often made him a villain in the eyes of authority figures, fans rallied behind his authenticity and rebellious spirit. Punk's ability to merge reality with kayfabe created a character who defied traditional labels, making him a standout figure in modern wrestling.

Randy Orton

Throughout his career, Randy Orton has seamlessly transitioned between hero and villain, often operating in a morally ambiguous space. His "Legend Killer" persona, while ruthless, was admired for its boldness and commitment. Even as a villain, Orton's in-ring skill and calculated demeanor earned him grudging respect from fans. His ability to adapt his character to suit the moment has made him one of wrestling's most enduring anti-heroes.

Concluding Thoughts

Anti-hero heels challenge the traditional boundaries of wrestling storytelling, proving that characters don't have to fit neatly into the roles of hero or villain to captivate audiences. By blending traits from both sides, these wrestlers create complex narratives that resonate with fans on a deeper level. These anti-heroes have redefined what it means to be a villain in professional wrestling, ensuring their place in the sport's storied history.

The Comedy Villain:

When Evil Was Played for Laughs

Not all wrestling villains are designed to inspire fear or hatred—some are created to make us laugh while still provoking boos. The comedy villain is a unique archetype, blending humor with underhanded tactics to entertain and frustrate audiences in equal measure. These characters may not dominate with brute strength or psychological mind games, but their antics ensure they remain unforgettable. Often used to lighten the mood or provide comic relief, comedy villains show that even bad guys can have a sense of humor—and that laughter can be a powerful storytelling tool in the wrestling world.

Santino Marella

Santino Marella's career was defined by his over-the-top antics and exaggerated arrogance, making him one of WWE's most memorable comedy villains. Whether wielding his infamous "Cobra" hand puppet or bumbling his way into matches he had no business winning, Marella's comedic timing was impeccable. His faux-serious promos, often delivered in his exaggerated Italian accent, made fans laugh while still rooting for his opponents. Santino's ability to blend humor with just enough villainy made him a fan-favorite heel.

The Miztourage (Curtis Axel and Bo Dallas)

As lackeys for The Miz, Curtis Axel and Bo Dallas embraced their roles as comedic villains who added levity to intense storylines. Their exaggerated devotion to The Miz and willingness to humiliate themselves for his approval drew laughter and jeers from fans. Whether failing spectacularly to assist The Miz during matches or delivering awkwardly over-the-top promos, The Miztourage perfectly embodied the comedic heel archetype, adding depth to Miz's villainous persona.

The Genius (Lanny Poffo)

The Genius, portrayed by Lanny Poffo, took arrogance and blended it with poetry and humor. Dressed in a graduation cap and gown, The Genius delivered rhyming promos that insulted his opponents and the audience with a smug, intellectual flair. His antics, such as prancing around the ring or outsmarting his opponents with comically sneaky tactics, made him a hilariously detestable character. Despite his comedic approach, The Genius's verbal dexterity and unique style left a lasting impression.

"Hollywood" Hogan and the nWo

While the nWo's inception was rooted in intimidation and dominance, their antics often veered into the realm of comedy. From spray-painting their opponents to mocking other wrestlers in over-the-top parody promos, "Hollywood" Hulk Hogan and his crew added a humorous edge to their villainy. One notable example was their infamous spoof of the Four Horsemen, where Kevin Nash's exaggerated impression of Arn Anderson left fans both laughing and seething. This blend of humor and menace helped keep the nWo fresh and entertaining.

Doink the Clown (Heel Version)

While Doink the Clown's early portrayal leaned into a darker, more sinister clown persona, his comedic side also shone through in his pranks and antics. Doink's ability to frustrate opponents with slapstick humor—like tripping them with banana peels or using trick props—made him a unique kind of villain. His blend of mischief and malice ensured that fans laughed even as they booed, cementing his place as one of wrestling's most unusual comedy heels.

Concluding Thoughts

Comedy villains bring a unique dynamic to professional wrestling, proving that even bad guys can make us laugh while driving the storyline forward. By entertaining audiences while keeping the heroes on their toes, comedy villains ensure that the world of wrestling remains as unpredictable as it is entertaining.

Beyond the Ring

Professional wrestling has always been larger than life, but its influence extends far beyond the confines of the squared circle. Wrestling villains, in particular, have left an indelible mark on pop culture, movies, video games, and even real-world interactions. Their ability to provoke emotions and create unforgettable moments has made them not just icons of the ring but also significant cultural figures. Whether they're starring in blockbuster films, appearing on the shelves as action figures, or drawing real-life ire from fans, these heels prove that their villainy knows no boundaries.

Wrestling villains have often served as a mirror of society, reflecting our fears, frustrations, and fascination with rebellion.

Heels of the Ring

From the dastardly deeds that made them famous to the ways they've transcended their roles to influence other forms of media, their impact is undeniable. Their personas have been immortalized in countless ways, from wrestling-themed movies like *No Holds Barred* to video games where players revel in the chance to step into the boots of their favorite bad guys. These chapters will explore how villains have shaped the wrestling landscape while also becoming cultural touchstones.

This section delves into the multifaceted legacy of wrestling's greatest heels beyond the ring. You'll discover how villains have dominated pop culture, and even faced real-world consequences for their actions. From merchandise that captures their essence to the interactions with fans that blurred the lines between performance and reality, this section celebrates the far-reaching influence of wrestling's most notorious figures.

Through these explorations, we'll see how wrestling villains have transcended their roles as mere antagonists to become legends whose impact resonates in unexpected ways. As you dive into these stories, you'll find that the villain's role isn't just about creating drama inside the ring—it's about leaving a legacy that stretches far beyond it.

Wrestling Villains in Pop Culture

Andre the Giant in *The Princess Bride*: Andre the Giant's portrayal of Fezzik in *The Princess Bride* showed a softer, comedic side to the legendary wrestler. Despite his villainous wrestling persona, Andre's kind-hearted giant character won over audiences worldwide. His role remains one of the most beloved examples of a wrestler crossing into pop culture.

Roddy Piper in *They Live:* "Rowdy" Roddy Piper starred as the lead in John Carpenter's cult classic *They Live*, playing a drifter uncovering a hidden alien conspiracy. While Piper often played a heel in wrestling, his role as a reluctant hero solidified his status as a pop culture icon. The film's line, "I have come here to chew bubblegum and kick ass, and I'm all out of bubblegum," has become legendary.

Hulk Hogan in *Rocky III*: Hulk Hogan's portrayal of Thunderlips in *Rocky III* showcased his over-the-top wrestling persona in a boxing movie. As the "Ultimate Male," Hogan's exaggerated villainy brought wrestling's theatrics to Hollywood. His memorable scenes with Sylvester Stallone helped bridge the gap between wrestling and mainstream entertainment.

The Iron Sheik's Viral Internet Presence: Decades after his in-ring career, The Iron Sheik became a pop culture sensation through his unfiltered and often outrageous social media posts. His fiery comments on modern wrestlers and humorous takes on life earned him a massive online following, cementing his legacy as a larger-than-life character.

The Undertaker in Paranormal Documentaries: Known for his eerie wrestling persona, The Undertaker has inspired numerous paranormal documentaries and references in horror-themed shows. His character's supernatural elements have made him a staple in discussions about wrestling's influence on pop culture's fascination with the macabre.

Macho Man Randy Savage as Bonesaw in *Spider-Man*: Randy Savage brought his signature intensity to the big screen as Bonesaw McGraw in Sam Raimi's *Spider-Man* (2002). His cameo as an aggressive wrestler facing off against Peter Parker in a steel cage became a fan-favorite moment that celebrated his larger-than-life wrestling persona.

The Rock's Hollywood Dominance: Although Dwayne "The Rock" Johnson is best known for his heroic roles, his time as a wrestling heel laid the foundation for his charismatic acting career. Films like *Fast & Furious* and *Jumanji* showcase his ability to play both villainous and heroic characters with equal charm, cementing his place as one of Hollywood's biggest stars.

Triple H's Cameo in *Blade: Trinity*: Triple H brought his imposing presence to the vampire-hunting genre in *Blade: Trinity*. Playing the role of a henchman, his character leaned into his wrestling villain roots, complete with brutal fight scenes and a dark sense of humor.

The nWo's Influence on Music and Fashion: The rebellious spirit of the nWo extended beyond wrestling, influencing the grunge and hip-hop scenes of the 1990s. Their black-and-white logo became a pop culture symbol, appearing on everything from music videos to streetwear, showcasing how wrestling villains can shape broader cultural trends.

Ric Flair's Catchphrases in Hip-Hop: Ric Flair's flamboyant lifestyle and iconic phrases like "Wooo!" have been immortalized in hip-hop music. Artists like Offset and Pusha T have referenced Flair in their lyrics, celebrating his impact as a cultural icon.

Kane in *See No Evil*: Kane's transition from the wrestling ring to horror films was seamless with his role as Jacob Goodnight in *See No Evil*. The movie capitalized on Kane's menacing presence, establishing him as a credible horror villain while keeping his wrestling roots intact.

Big Show in *The Waterboy*: Big Show's comedic turn as Captain Insano in Adam Sandler's *The Waterboy* showcased his ability to blend humor with his intimidating presence. The role became a cult favorite, reflecting wrestling's crossover appeal in mainstream comedy.

Becky Lynch in *Young Rock*: Becky Lynch's guest appearance as Cyndi Lauper in the TV show *Young Rock* highlighted wrestling's connection to pop culture history. Her performance paid homage to the Rock 'n' Wrestling Era, blending nostalgia with her modern-day wrestling stardom.

Sasha Banks in *The Mandalorian*: Sasha Banks expanded her reach into pop culture with her role as Koska Reeves in *The Mandalorian*. Her performance brought wrestling's physicality and charisma to the Star Wars universe, highlighting how wrestlers can seamlessly transition into mainstream entertainment.

Randy Savage's Slim Jim Campaign: "Snap into a Slim Jim!" became one of the most iconic advertising campaigns of the 1990s, thanks to Randy Savage's energetic delivery. His over-the-top persona made the commercials unforgettable, cementing his place as a pop culture icon beyond wrestling.

Villains in Wrestling Movies and TV Shows

Hulk Hogan in *No Holds Barred*: Starring as Rip Thomas, Hogan faced off against the villainous Zeus, played by Tiny Lister, in this over-the-top wrestling movie. While the film was not a critical success, Zeus's menacing persona made an impact, even crossing over into WWE storylines where he continued to feud with Hogan.

The Rock in *Fighting with My Family*: In this biographical film about Paige's rise to WWE fame, Dwayne "The Rock"

Johnson made a cameo, blending his real-life persona with his wrestling past. His scene highlighted his charisma and ability to inspire both fans and wrestlers, demonstrating his ongoing connection to wrestling's cinematic ventures.

Roddy Piper in *Tagteam*: Piper teamed with Jesse Ventura in this TV pilot about former wrestlers who become crime-fighting detectives. Although the series wasn't picked up, the unique concept showcased the potential for wrestling villains to take their personas into action-packed television roles.

Triple H in *The Chaperone*: Playing an ex-convict trying to reconnect with his daughter, Triple H showed a softer side in this family-friendly movie. While not a villain in this role, his reputation as a wrestling heel added an interesting layer to his performance.

Randy Savage in *Walker, Texas Ranger*: Appearing as a guest star, Randy Savage played a wrestling villain who brought his larger-than-life personality to the small screen. His intense performance and ability to stay in character reflected his wrestling roots, even in a non-wrestling context.

The Miz in *The Marine 3: Homefront:* The Miz transitioned from wrestling to action movies with his role in *The Marine* franchise. While his character is a hero, his natural charisma and experience as a wrestling villain gave his performance an edge, proving his versatility as an entertainer.

Big Show in *Jingle All the Way:* As a giant mall Santa, Big Show's brief but memorable role showcased his comedic timing and physical presence. While not a traditional villain, his imposing size and antics played into the larger-than-life roles often associated with wrestling heels.

Steve Austin in *The Longest Yard:* "Stone Cold" Steve Austin's role as a sadistic prison guard in this football-themed comedy leaned into his wrestling persona's tougher, villainous traits. His ability to deliver menacing lines and physical intimidation made his character stand out.

Edge in *Haven*: Adam "Edge" Copeland's recurring role in the supernatural drama *Haven* showcased his versatility as an actor. Playing a complex character with both heroic and villainous traits, Edge used his wrestling experience to add depth to his performance.

Goldberg in *The Flash*: Bill Goldberg guest-starred in the popular TV series as Big Sir, a misunderstood character with incredible strength. Though not a villain in the traditional sense, Goldberg's intimidating presence added an edge to the role.

Batista in *Spectre*: As Mr. Hinx in the James Bond film *Spectre*, Dave Batista brought a silent but deadly menace to the screen. His wrestling background helped him deliver intense fight scenes, cementing his place as a memorable cinematic villain.

CM Punk in *Heels*: Punk's role in the wrestling-themed drama *Heels* allowed him to explore the nuances of wrestling villainy.

His performance captured the complexity of wrestling personas, blurring the lines between character and reality.

Kevin Nash in *Magic Mike*: Kevin Nash's role in *Magic Mike* showcased his ability to adapt to unexpected genres. While not a villain, his larger-than-life presence and charisma reflected the traits that made him a standout in wrestling.

Ric Flair in *Baywatch*: Flair guest-starred in an episode of *Baywatch*, playing an exaggerated version of himself. His over-the-top antics and signature "Wooo!" made for a memorable appearance that highlighted his crossover appeal.

Mick Foley in *The Peanut Butter Falcon*: Foley's role as a wrestling promoter in this heartwarming indie film drew on his real-life experience in the industry. His ability to blend humor and sincerity added depth to the movie's exploration of wrestling culture.

The nWo in *Ready to Rumble*: Featuring members of the nWo, this wrestling-themed comedy leaned into the group's villainous legacy. Their larger-than-life personas added authenticity to the film, making it a cult favorite among wrestling fans.

Merchandising the Villain:

Toys, Shirts, and More

nWo Merchandise Revolution: The New World Order's black-and-white logo became one of the most iconic symbols in wrestling history. From T-shirts to bandanas, nWo merchandise was a must-have for fans during the faction's peak, selling millions of items worldwide and setting a new standard for wrestling merchandise.

The Undertaker's Action Figures: The Undertaker's dark persona translated perfectly into action figure form, with toys featuring his signature trench coat, hat, and even miniature caskets. These collectibles became staples for wrestling fans, highlighting his status as a merchandising powerhouse.

"Austin 3:16" and Heel Memorabilia: While Stone Cold Steve Austin became a beloved anti-hero, his early heel run helped make "Austin 3:16" one of the best-selling wrestling shirts of all time. The shirt's rebellious message resonated with fans, blurring the lines between hero and villain.

"Macho Man" Randy Savage Slim Jim Campaign: Randy Savage's partnership with Slim Jim extended beyond the ring, with his "Snap into a Slim Jim!" tagline appearing on posters, packaging, and commercials. The campaign's success turned Savage into a pop culture icon, proving the marketability of wrestling villains.

The Fiend's Masks and Lanterns: Bray Wyatt's "The Fiend" character inspired chilling merchandise, including replica masks and his eerie lantern. These items became instant collectibles, emphasizing The Fiend's appeal as a modern horror-inspired wrestling villain.

Vince McMahon's "No Chance in Hell" Shirt: Vince McMahon's villainous persona as the evil boss was immortalized in merchandise like his "No Chance in Hell" T-shirt. Fans loved to hate him, making his gear a popular choice for those who appreciated his antagonistic character.

Ric Flair Robes and Accessories: Ric Flair's extravagant robes became iconic symbols of his heel persona, leading to high-end replicas for fans. Flair's catchphrases, such as "Wooo!", also appeared on shirts, ensuring his legacy extended into merchandising.

The Miz's "Haters Love Me" Line: The Miz capitalized on his arrogant persona with the "Haters Love Me" merchandise line. From shirts to hats, his gear played into his heel antics, allowing fans to embrace their love-hate relationship with his character.

The Iron Sheik's Retro Resurgence: Decades after his prime, The Iron Sheik's merchandise, including shirts with his infamous phrases, saw a resurgence thanks to his viral social media presence. His classic heel persona proved timeless in the merchandising world.

Edge's "Rated R Superstar" Gear: Edge's edgy, villainous persona led to the creation of "Rated R Superstar" merchandise, including shirts, hats, and posters. His gear became synonymous with his rebellious heel character.

Jake "The Snake" Roberts' Snake Accessories: Jake Roberts's association with snakes extended to his merchandise, including snake-themed shirts and action figures. His unique gimmick made his items stand out among wrestling collectibles.

Brock Lesnar's "Eat, Sleep, Conquer, Repeat" Line: Brock Lesnar's dominance as a heel was immortalized in his "Eat, Sleep, Conquer, Repeat" merchandise. The straightforward message captured his no-nonsense persona, making it a top seller.

CM Punk's "Best in the World" Merchandise: Although often portrayed as an anti-hero, Punk's rebellious nature made his "Best in the World" gear a hit. His heelish confidence resonated with fans, leading to strong sales across multiple items.

Real-Life Jail Time:

Villains Who Broke the Law

The Iron Sheik and Hacksaw Jim Duggan's Arrest: In 1987, The Iron Sheik and Hacksaw Jim Duggan were arrested together after being caught with marijuana and alcohol while driving. The incident shocked fans as it revealed a real-life camaraderie between two in-ring enemies. While Duggan faced minor repercussions, The Iron Sheik's image as a villain intensified due to the scandal.

Abdullah the Butcher and Health Violations: Legendary hardcore wrestler Abdullah the Butcher faced legal action over claims that he knowingly spread Hepatitis C to other wrestlers. The allegations led to a tarnished reputation and a court judgment against him, adding a dark chapter to his storied career.

Hardbody Harrison and Human Trafficking Charges: Former WCW wrestler Hardbody Harrison was sentenced to life in prison after being convicted of human trafficking and forced labor charges. His heinous crimes shocked the wrestling world and underscored the potential for real-life villainy to surpass anything seen in the ring.

Nick Gage's Bank Robbery: Deathmatch wrestler Nick Gage was arrested and sentenced to five years in prison for robbing a bank in 2011. Gage's legal troubles added an edge of authenticity to his already hardcore persona, making his eventual return to wrestling all the more compelling for fans.

New Jack's Assault Charges: Known for his violent in-ring style, New Jack faced legal consequences after a match in 2004 where he severely injured his opponent with a weapon. His reputation as one of wrestling's most dangerous performers only grew after the incident.

Randy Orton's AWOL Incident: Before becoming one of WWE's top stars, Randy Orton served time in a military prison for going AWOL during his stint in the Marines. This real-life rebellion added a layer of authenticity to his early "Legend Killer" heel persona.

Terry Funk's Bar Brawl Incident: Hardcore legend Terry Funk once found himself in legal trouble after a bar fight escalated into an all-out brawl. Though charges were eventually dropped, the incident added to Funk's reputation as a tough-as-nails performer both inside and outside the ring.

Hulk Hogan's Legal Battles: While not criminal, Hulk Hogan's involvement in lawsuits, including his high-profile case against Gawker, showcased the darker side of celebrity life.

Heels of the Ring

His legal battles often reflected the larger-than-life drama of his wrestling career.

Fan Interactions: When the Hate Got Real

Roddy Piper Attacked by Fans with Knives: Roddy Piper's knack for taunting audiences made him a frequent target of violent fans. During one infamous incident in the 1980s, Piper narrowly avoided being stabbed while leaving the ring, forcing WWE to employ additional security measures to protect him from such attacks.

Iron Sheik and Death Threats: The Iron Sheik's portrayal of an anti-American heel during a time of geopolitical tension led to numerous death threats being mailed to him. At one event, a fan attempted to breach security to confront him directly, believing his villainous character to be real.

Freddie Blassie's Car Tires Slashed: Freddie Blassie's sharp-tongued promos and in-ring antics incited such hatred that fans slashed his car tires after a show in the 1960s. Security had to escort him out of the arena to prevent further escalation from the furious crowd.

Sgt. Slaughter's Iraqi Sympathizer Gimmick: Sgt. Slaughter's controversial heel turn during the Gulf War sparked outrage, with one fan throwing a brick through his car window. The intense backlash required increased security around his home and at events where he performed.

Jake "The Snake" Roberts and the Damien Incident: In a memorable 1980s match, a fan attempted to climb the barricade to free Jake Roberts's python, Damien, from its bag, mistakenly believing the snake was in danger. Security restrained the fan before the situation escalated further.

Heels of the Ring

Vince McMahon Pelted with Trash: During the Attitude Era, Vince McMahon's "evil boss" character drew such ire that fans regularly threw cups, bottles, and even chairs at him. At one pay-per-view, the amount of debris hurled into the ring delayed the show as cleanup crews worked to clear the area.

Triple H and Fan Interference: At a live show in the early 2000s, a fan jumped into the ring during a promo by Triple H, attempting to tackle him. Triple H quickly subdued the intruder until security arrived, maintaining his composure and using the incident to further his heel persona.

Bobby Heenan Pummeled with Drinks: Bobby "The Brain" Heenan's snarky commentary and ringside antics often provoked fans to hurl drinks and popcorn at him. At one event, Heenan had to change his suit mid-show after being soaked by an irate audience member.

Chris Jericho and the Parking Lot Incident: In 2009, Chris Jericho confronted a group of fans who blocked his car and shouted obscenities at him. The altercation turned physical when one fan tried to grab him, leading to a chaotic scene before venue security intervened.

The Dudley Boyz and Riots: During an ECW event, The Dudley Boyz' inflammatory promo led to fans throwing dozens of chairs into the ring. The chaos escalated to the point where wrestlers and staff had to clear the ring to prevent injuries.

Andy Kaufman and Jerry Lawler Feud: Andy Kaufman's provocations during his feud with Jerry Lawler included mocking fans and insulting Memphis culture. At one match, a fan threw a chair into the ring, narrowly missing Kaufman as security rushed to calm the crowd.

Hulk Hogan's nWo Turn Reaction: After Hulk Hogan revealed himself as the leader of the nWo at Bash at the Beach 1996, fans bombarded the ring with trash. The sheer volume of debris delayed the event, with staff needing several minutes to clear the ring for the next segment.

"Ladies and gentlemen, this is Jett Clark stepping into the ring one last time! If this book body-slammed your boredom and delivered a knockout punch of entertainment, let your voice be heard!

Head over to Amazon and drop an honest review. Your feedback is the championship belt we strive for!"

Made in the USA
Middletown, DE
30 July 2025